Love Before Sex

How to Establish Love and Commitment Before Bringing Sex Into the Relationship

Laurie Gelfand, Ph.D.

Love Before Sex:
How to Establish Love and Commitment Before Bringing Sex Into the Relationship

Copyright © 2013 by Laurie Gelfand, Ph.D.

www.LoveBeforeSex.com

ALL RIGHTS RESERVED

No part of this publication may be reproduced, stored in a retrieval system or transmitted, in any form or by any means—electronic, mechanical, photocopying, recording or otherwise—without prior written permission, except for the inclusion of brief quotations in a review.

ISBN: **978-1491252901**

First Edition
Printed in the United States of America

This book was originally published under the title, *If It's Love You Want, Why Settle For Just Sex?: The 10 Most Common Mistakes Women Make and How to Avoid Them* (Prima, 1996), and under the author's maiden name, Laurie Langford. While much of the material is the same, this new version represents a substantial, more secular redraft containing new material and several new stories. The names have been changed to protect the identities of those interviewed.

Also by Laurie Langford:

The Big Talk: Talking to Your Child About Sex and Dating
(John Wiley & Sons, 1998)

All of the stories are real people, interviewed by Dr. Laurie Gelfand.

I dedicate this book to my amazing husband, Michael.

Thank you for teaching me how to love,

for loving me unconditionally,

and for being the best part of my life,

Love, *all ways.*

Table of Contents

My Story   vii

Questions   xiii

Introduction   xv

Chapter 1:
Love is the Goal   1

Chapter 2:
How Sex Before Love Sabotages True Love   29

Chapter 3:
The Pre-Sex Pow-Wow: What to Say and How to Say it   57

Chapter 4:
Responding to His Advances without Bruising His Ego   77

Chapter 5:
How Far Can You Go?   91

Chapter 6:
But I'm so *Randy*! What's a Girl to Do?   109

Chapter 7:
Starting Over if You've Already Gone too Far   119

Chapter 8:
Getting a Commitment   135

Chapter 9:
What You Need to Know About Him Before 147
Getting Physical

Chapter 10:
The Art of Awakening Love 173

Chapter 11:
Increase Self-Esteem 199

Chapter 12:
The Qualities Men Find Most Irresistible in 217
a Lifetime Mate

Chapter 13:
Getting a Marriage Proposal 229

Chapter 14:
The 10 Most Common Mistakes Women 237
Make

Chapter 15:
Being a Great Lover for Life 259

About the Author 263

MY STORY
WHY I WROTE THIS BOOK

I originally wrote this book back in 1996, under the title *If It's Love You Want, Why Settle for Just Sex? The 10 Most Common Mistakes Women Make and How to Avoid Them* (Prima, 1996). The book was published in several languages; I conducted seminars and workshops throughout the United States, and went on many national television and radio shows. At the time, I hadn't received my education (I now have a Ph.D. in clinical psychology), nor was I married. I simply had a deep desire to help women learn the most important principles related to dating and building a relationship. The basic message is essentially the same in this new version of the book, although I changed the title and added a few new sections. I attempted to modernize the message without losing its essence. I am also happily married today, as a result of applying the principles in the book. I am living proof that they really do work!

Now that almost 18 years have passed, I felt the book still had tremendous potential, and I also felt strongly that I could make it an even better book. What really drove me to reintroduce the book to society was re-reading the letters I received from women all over the world, as well as the many women (and men) I have worked with over the years. These women reminded me of the tremendous pain and heartache that so many women are experiencing as a result of not

Love Before Sex

understanding the sexual aspect of a relationship—meaning, when it's okay to bring sex into the relationship, and what to discuss prior to doing so. It is my hope that this updated version of the book will reach even more women, and that it will alleviate some of the suffering that I know still exists today.

This pain often begins when we are very young. One of my first memories of making out with a boy is also one of my most painful memories to this day. I was in the 6th grade and a group of kids met up at a boy's house. One of the boys who had been eyeing me for some time walked over and started talking to me. We chatted for a bit and then he took my hand and led me into one of the bedrooms and shut the door. We sat on the bed and he started kissing me. I had never kissed a boy before and I was amazed at the intense feelings that overcame me. Butterflies in the stomach, a wave of heat flashed through me as if I was on fire. I had never felt anything like this before and it was incredible. His hand moved to my small, still-developing breast. I was scared and knew I probably should stop him but the feeling was so amazing I didn't want it to stop. It was then that my father showed up at the house looking for me and I had to go. I jumped up and ran out the door.

The next day at school I was so excited to see the boy. I made sure to wear something extra special to look my best and I scanned the halls when I walked in the building. There he was, with a couple of his friends, laughing and talking. I walked towards him and caught his eye. I was about to say hello but I noticed the total disdain in his eyes. He rejected me so completely with just one look, and it felt like someone slugged me in the stomach. When I went to class I kept going over it in my mind. How could he treat me that way? After

My Story

what we did? We were so close—so tender—the actions were so loving, or so it seemed. Didn't he care about me at all? It baffled me and hurt me deeply. I had never felt so alone or so abandoned. It was then that I learned that boys are often very interested in getting what they want from you, but that doesn't necessarily mean they care about you.

I wish I could say I learned from that one experience, but I was young and impetuous and I thought maybe it was just that particular boy who was a jerk. Many more painful lessons followed. All of these experiences led me to the writing of this book; in the hopes that it could possibly spare women some of the pain I endured as a result of my lack of awareness and knowledge.

I was single for a long time and spent many years afraid that I would never meet the right guy. I struggled to understand men, the dating process, how two people fall in love, and how to make a relationship last. I especially wanted to better understand the *sexual* aspect of a relationship because it seemed to me that sex changed everything. Once I became sexual the entire dynamic of the relationship seemed to shift and I ended up feeling so much more vulnerable, unlike the men, who seemed to be more in control at that point. I, like so many of you reading this, wanted to be loved, adored, cherished, respected, and I wanted the man I was with to want to spend the rest of his life with me. It didn't make sense to me that we would be in a sexual relationship and yet the relationship didn't progress in the expected way—from dating to marriage. It seemed that my "relationships" felt more like "situations"—whereby it looked like a romantic relationship, but the feelings were severely underdeveloped and a solid foundation was lacking. No surprise that my "situations" always ended after a year or two, with serial monogamy being my apparent modus operandi. I didn't know how to break the cycle, but I had a hunch that it had to do with when sex appears on the scene, since that is when everything changed. I knew that I felt more in control *prior* to becoming sexual, and completely out of control once we did become sexual. It seemed that the men aggressively pursued me up until we had sex, and then their attitude changed afterwards. I now know that this was simply because their feelings for me had not developed enough, and therefore they weren't fully committed to me. I allowed things to move forward too soon because I didn't know what my standards were, or how to implement them. I didn't know how to pace a relationship or that it was even my job to do so.

I had a couple of serious relationships in which we stayed together for a couple of years and a few "I love you's" were exchanged—but I could tell that the *depth* of emotion and commitment was not there. Something was missing. I felt alone, lost, frustrated, and afraid. I was afraid that I would never figure this out, and I was getting close to believing that I may not even be lovable. There must be something wrong with *me*, I thought.

I was so tired of this vicious cycle, of one wrong relationship after another that I began to take stock of my life. I read every self-help book on the market and I began studying successful relationships that I admired. I began to develop my own little formula, if you will, for how to approach relationships (the contents of this book). I made a commitment to myself that I would never settle for less than what I wanted. That was the end of my sexually-based dead-end relationships. I felt a renewed sense of confidence, knowing that I was armed with a process that would get me the kind of relationship I wanted.

My Story

All I ever wanted was to be deeply loved by a good man. I wanted him to cherish me, adore me. I wanted the fairy tale! And after many years of struggling and attempting to figure out and apply the principles in this book, I finally got what I always wanted. My friends always tell me that they want the kind of marriage Michael and I have, and I am so grateful that I finally got it right. He is perfect for me in so many ways, but mostly because he is so loving, unselfish, and accepting of me and my flaws. <u>This is something that I learned about love: when a man truly loves you, he finds even your flaws adorable on some level.</u> He rolls with your idiosyncrasies because he loves you that much. You don't have to perfect, you are able to be yourself. It's the most amazing feeling—to have someone care so much about you and want to spend the rest of his life with you. Anyone can get married. Lots of people do, and many also get divorced. Many people marry and they are not even in love! It isn't about getting married—it's about developing passionate, solid, real love that can last a lifetime. It's about knowing how to pace the relationship and how to awaken these feelings of love in the man of your choice, and how to ensure that the condition of the relationship is completely right before walking down that aisle. It really is all up to you. You hold the keys, you have the power. It is all based on some simple principles that are not always so easy to apply. But if you apply them and stick to these guidelines throughout the entire process without giving in too soon along the way, I promise that you will be so grateful you did.

WHAT DO YOU THINK?

WHEN IS IT OKAY TO BRING SEX INTO A NEW RELATIONSHIP?

- ☐ Whenever each person feels like it.
- ☐ Just not on the first date.
- ☐ Just not on the first, second, or third date.
- ☐ After several weeks.
- ☐ After several months.
- ☐ When it feels right.
- ☐ If they use protection and aren't seeing other people.
- ☐ When the woman has a ring and a date.
- ☐ After they are married.

Introduction

The responses I get when I ask the question on the previous page are very interesting. *It depends,* is the most common retort, followed by a litany of qualifiers, based on age, what's going on in your life, what you want in the moment, and who you're with. It is clearly a complicated matter, and one that I find many women uncomfortable discussing. Why? Because the subject triggers all kinds of emotions—many of which can be quite painful—like shame, fear, uncertainty, embarrassment, guilt, anger, confusion, and so on. Women don't want to admit that they may have slept with a guy too soon, or that they were devastated or embarrassed when he didn't call after they had a romp in the sack. Many women have suffered from sexual abuse and trauma, so the subject can conjure up painful memories and emotions. Many women simply haven't thought about when it's okay to have sex, they are unclear about their sexual values, and they wing it in their dating experiences. "Winging it" is exactly what this book attempts to prevent. Rather than going with the flow and finding yourself in over your head (or flat on your back!) when you are just getting to know someone, this book will enable you to become crystal clear as to when it is okay to be sexual, what to say when he makes a sexual advance, and how to pace the entire relationship from meeting him to inspiring a marriage proposal.

Love Before Sex

I am going to ask you to look at relationships in a different way. You may not be used to viewing the dating process and relationships through the prism of the *sexual* aspect of the relationship. You may think that sex is just one part of a relationship and that it isn't such a big deal. But please read with an open mind and try to see relationships from my perspective. Instead of viewing sex as perhaps an innocuous part of any relationship, consider that there might be a lot more to it than you might think. I truly believe that if you fully understand the seriousness of the sexual aspect of a relationship and approach your dating life with that in mind, you will be amazed at how differently things go for you.

Casual Sex

When to have sex for the first time in a new relationship is one of the most, if not *the* most, important decisions you will make and your decision plays a crucial role in the future success, or failure of that relationship. It can have a major impact on the quality and depth of the emotional connection the two of you share. Here is a quick run-down of just some the potential hazards of sex too soon: it can turn a guy off and scare him away (so unfair, I know), you can get emotionally attached to a jerk or someone who isn't right for you, you can thwart the falling-in-love process and end up with a watered-down version of the real thing, and you lose control and give away your power. All of this typically leads to a lot of emotional pain. Many of you reading this already know what I'm talking about. Whether you have witnessed it with others or have experienced it yourself: casual sex is risky business and it rarely gives you what you

Introduction

really want, which is a good man who loves you so much he wants to spend the rest of his life with you.

Various Scenarios

There are a couple of sad scenarios that I see time and time again. First is the woman who simply can't contain herself—maybe she had too much to drink, or she was swept off her feet by his intoxicating words—in any case, she ended up having sex on the first, second, or first few dates, and as a result, she never hears from the guy again. Or maybe she hears from him for a time but the relationship never really develops into anything solid. She may realize she made a mistake, and either she lowers her head in shame and avoids seeing her friends who know about it, or she flippantly announces that he wasn't her type anyway, or that she just did it for her own pleasure, or that he was just a jerk. Regardless, if she's at all in touch with her feelings, deep down she experiences the cringe, the remorse, the hurt that comes with feeling used and foolish.

The other scenario is the woman who is in a full-fledged relationship with someone—perhaps even with a solid commitment to be exclusive—but who can't quite get the guy to take it to the next level (marriage). She is frustrated, angry, annoyed, and fit-to-be-tied. She can't understand why, if he says he loves her (maybe he won't even say it), and they have been together for a fair amount of time, he won't pop the question. If she brings up the subject she's made to feel as if she's pressuring him. She gets tired of the same old excuses: It's too soon to talk about marriage, I'm just not ready, I need to get my finances in order, and on it goes. The months and years roll by, with her thinking of little else and wondering what she did

Love Before Sex

wrong. The fact is she is stuck in a stagnating relationship that may or may not ever lead to marriage, but that obviously did not develop properly from the start. She may have done everything else right, <u>but having sex before he developed feelings for her and made a commitment prevented his feelings from being able to progress naturally.</u>

Pauline, 49, expressed her feelings about being in this predicament. "I am so sick and tired of these relationships that last anywhere from one month to several years, but that don't seem to be the real deal. I always thought I had a bad picker, but now I'm thinking that maybe I do get sexually involved too soon. The relationships are never strong enough to withstand the challenges that always come along eventually."

Obviously relationships are complicated and failed or stagnating relationships are not always the result of having sex too soon. But the fact is if you develop a solid *foundation* of love before having sex, your chances of the relationship moving forward to marriage increases dramatically, and your relationship is more solid in general. How could it not be?

What You Get When You Put Love Before Sex

As a woman, you have the power. It is unfortunate that so many women give their power away! Men want sex and they will go to great lengths to get it (testosterone is a powerful little hormone). And you hold all the cards as you deny his requests for sex. Putting love before sex sets you apart from all the other women who are too afraid, or unknowledgeable, or unskilled when it comes to what to say

Introduction

and do with the sexual aspect of a relationship, or who reject the wisdom in this approach. You immediately appear to be different and refreshing to men. You create a challenge and an excitement that the man cannot easily dismiss. You may not be as beautiful or thin or successful as the other women who "put out", but you are what trumps all of those qualities: *unattainable.* He immediately realizes to himself, "Hmmm... I'm going to have to take this one seriously." He will be forced to stand up to attention (so to speak) and consider how he truly feels about you, and what future potential there might be with you. This is what you want to have happen because you aren't willing to sacrifice months or years with the wrong guy, as you may have done in the past.

Resistance

Are you one of those women who says, "But men will never put up with that!"? If so, you have been giving in sexually way too soon based on a faulty premise. You think that if you don't have sex with him when he makes an advance, or very early on in the dating process, that he will lose interest and not stick around. You may not have even been conscious of this at the time. But if you have been in several relationships in which the men never seem to get to the point where they want to marry you, I would like to suggest that this is a big part of why that is the case. You may have been blaming the men or any other myriad of reasons. But if you make the decision right now to stop having sex before love is established, I promise you will notice a huge difference in your dating life.

Men will wait. They will honor your feelings and they will be intrigued. And the ones that won't? You don't want them anyway!

Love Before Sex

Maybe you feel like Lucy, 24. She is frustrated and annoyed with the double standard that still exists in our culture because she wants to be able to have sex without having to take it slow. She said, "Why do I need to wait on having sex only because it might make this guy lose sight of how great I am? Why should I deny my needs for someone else?!" I see her point and I feel her pain. There are countless women out there who feel the same way. I can tell you that it is *not* my goal to set back the clock, dilute Women's Rights, or limit your potential in any way. In fact, I want to *increase* your potential and give you the tools to create whatever life you want. Unfortunately, we have to deal with this pesky little double standard, which will require you to keep your clothes on for longer than perhaps you would like. But hey, you get love, commitment, adoration, and a lifetime mate out of it. Sounds like a deal to me!

Or maybe you're like Carly, 31. "I have never been one to have sex early on in a relationship. My mother taught me all about not giving it away too soon. But my problem is I just can't seem to find the right guy. They all end up being something other than what they presented in the beginning." As I dug deeper with Carly, I realized that her definition of sex too soon was different from mine, and that she did, in fact, have sex too soon based on my criteria. The men she dated were not in love with her before having sex with her; parameters for the relationship were not clearly established; and she didn't get to know them well enough before bringing sex into the equation. In her mind she was waiting a "reasonable" period of time, based on modern standards and what her friends were doing. Because she wasn't seen as a "loose" girl who peeled off

Introduction

her clothes on the first or second dates she felt she was handling that aspect of the situation well. But she wasn't following the message in this book—she was incorporating some of the ideas, but she wasn't doing it all and she didn't fully understand the process of how men fall in love.

Love Before Sex isn't just about saying no to sex for a specific amount of time. It is about empowering yourself to create the relationship of your dreams with the man of your choice by learning how to awaken deep feelings of love in him. It's about learning how to pace the relationship, keeping it on track and knowing when it's right or if it's time to let go and move on (which should happen *before* you have sex so that you can move on more easily).

Exceptions

We all know of exceptions to the rule. No doubt you have a friend, or cousin, or sister who slept with her partner on the first, second, or third date and they fell blissfully in love and have been happily married ever since. But it is definitely the *exception* to the rule. Why take such a huge risk when it comes to something so important?

There are plenty of reasons to balk at this approach: you're horny and want sex, you're afraid you'll lose the guy or that men in general won't put up with this, you can't contain the passion in the moment, you don't want to be seen as playing games or being manipulative, you don't have the patience, you don't believe it's necessary, you respond to sex more like a guy and don't get emotionally attached, or you're willing to take your chances on scaring men away by having sex too soon because it is all just too much work otherwise. All of these objections and more will be thoroughly examined

Love Before Sex

in the following pages. We will dissect the pros and cons, and by the time you finish reading this book you will clearly understand why you need to wait, how to do it, and you will have the tools you will need to create the kind of love you want.

What this Book Is and What it Isn't

Love Before Sex is a practical guide for single women of all ages. When this topic comes up, most people think it's only for young women and teens. Not so! This book is for women of *all* ages—it's for anyone who wants to build a real relationship and avoid having sex too soon.

The message is not based on religious values, or any type of morality. You may be atheist, agnostic, Jewish, Christian, Buddhist, or anything else for that matter. This isn't a conservative message nor is it about denying your natural sexual desires (temporarily delaying sex isn't going to kill you!). It also isn't about playing games or being manipulative. It is about embracing your power as a woman, learning how the falling-in-love process works, and getting what you want out of life. It's about taking control of your life and taking care of yourself so you don't get sidetracked for months or years with someone who doesn't really love you. It's about ending the cycle/pattern of dead-end relationships that are unfulfilling and unsatisfying. It is about creating the kind of love you have always wanted. Read on and enjoy!

Chapter 1
LOVE IS THE GOAL

The wonderful reality we enjoy today as women is that, for the most part, we can choose the way we want to live. We can marry or not, have children or not, have careers or be stay-at-home moms. We can have casual sex or we can even wait until we are married to become sexual, if that's what we want. We have *choices*, and from my perspective there is no right or wrong way to live as long as you live with integrity and do your best to not hurt yourself or others.

However, one thing that most people on the planet desire, above all else, is *love*. To love and to be loved. Most people want marriage, even though individuals are choosing to marry later these days. If you purchased this book I'm assuming you want love. And not just mediocre, run-of-the-mill love—you want the deepest, most real and lasting love possible.

In this chapter I am going to describe the kind of love that, while it may be rare, does exist. And if it exists, why can't it exist for you? Before you can make anything happen you have to have a vision, a goal. Create a vision board if that would inspire you. Write it all out in your journal. Use Siri to dictate it on your iPhone in your notes so you can periodically review it as you're sitting in a cab or on a

Love Before Sex

train. Never lose sight of what you want and never, ever settle for less.

To begin with, you want a good man. I know that the "bad boys" can be sexy, tall is nice, and a full head of hair might be important to you—but look at your friends and family members who have great marriages and wonderful husbands and see if they measure up to the physical specimens you've been angling for. The fact is, some of the best men are short, bald, and pudgy (I just described my husband, and all my single friends want someone just like him because he's such a great guy!). The point is, looks are not the most important thing and if they have been for you, and yet you have found yourself seriously disappointed in love, then you might want to reconsider your criteria. Looks fade—we all know that. Even the most attractive people become unattractive if they treat you badly and/or you can't trust them.

Having said that—I do know that there are plenty of wonderful good-looking men out there who would make great partners—so you don't have to give up on the idea of finding a hot guy with whom to connect. Just make sure they also have all of the character qualities, and don't rule out the short, bald, pudgy ones!

The most important thing is to find a man with impeccable integrity, a big heart, a kind soul. Someone who will be there for you no matter what and who loves even your flaws. He is the person you would want to call first whether something good or bad happens in your day. He's the one who will listen to you go and on, even if it's not the most exciting topic to him (although, even the best guys have their limits!). He is the one who laughs at your jokes and loves your mind. He's proud of you and can't wait to

Chapter 1 Love Is The Goal

introduce you to his family, friends, co-workers. It's obvious to everyone that he adores you and he's willing to shout it from the rooftops.

You can be yourself with this man—you're never afraid that he's going to be critical of you or not approve. You can be silly and giddy, or grumpy and blue—either way, he accepts you and it's okay. He wants to touch you, hold you, caress your hair and face, and stare into your beautiful eyes. He smiles lovingly at you when you talk and finds you utterly charming.

There is nothing quite like having a good man love you—you feel safe, secure, warm, happy. It's a wonderful feeling to know you can trust this one person explicitly because he has your best interests in mind. He responds to you differently than he responds to everyone else. He may be harsh with others, but with you he is tender and gentle. He cares about your welfare—physically, financially, emotionally, on all levels in fact. He wants to make sure your tires are in good shape and that you are not walking alone at night to your car. It isn't a problem for him to make sacrifices for you because he loves you! He is willing to put up with lunch with your crazy aunt or whatever the event might be—because he has made a commitment to be there for you, whatever that entails. And besides that, he just loves being with you.

Helen Andelin, author of the best-selling book *Fascinating Womanhood*, describes this as *celestial* love. She points out that even though a man might say, "I love you" to the woman in his life, do nice things for her, or remember her birthday, this doesn't necessarily constitute celestial love. She writes, "Celestial love is more intense, more spontaneous, and dynamic than passive actions... when

Love Before Sex

a man loves with his heart, he experiences a deep feeling within. It has been described as a feeling almost like pain. He may feel enchanted and fascinated. In addition, he feels a tender desire to protect and shelter the woman he loves from all harm, danger, and difficulty. Then there is the deeper, more spiritual feeling almost like worship."

One of the best examples of true, romantic love is of my mother and father-in-law. Married 59 years, they still behave like love-birds. The way he gently kisses her and says, "Good morning, my love" when she comes down for breakfast in the morning. The way they light up when they see each other, and laugh at the other's funny lines. They still go to the movies together every Sunday and even blush when teased about their still-active sex life. Their physical attraction has carried on all these years, as well as their emotional love and mutual adoration. Their relationship is the one that their many friends refer to when discussing true love.

I am fortunate to have married a man who had this as his model growing up. We like to think our relationship is similar to theirs. The best decision I ever made was to marry my husband, Michael, who makes me feel loved and adored every day. Actually, the best decision I ever made was to apply the principles in this book in our dating so that he developed the feelings of love for me that he has to this day! I was also incredibly lucky that I found a man with real integrity and a huge heart.

Take a good look at the people around you—family, friends, acquaintances, and even relationships in the movies. Consider if you would want what they have. Can you discern which of the men are truly and deeply in love with their spouses? What is the difference? I am not

Chapter 1 Love Is The Goal

suggesting that love never changes and that you can sustain the level of passion and heart-thumping romance and intimacy that you have when you begin dating and falling in love. But I do think it's important to have a clear vision of what being loved/cherished/adored looks like and how you want it to be for you. We all know the power of visualization. If you haven't already met your Prince Charming, start getting excited today about the possibilities and begin to visualize the man you want to come into your life and what your relationship will look and feel like when he does.

Love Creates Security in a Relationship

Women need to feel secure in a relationship and love is the foundation that creates that feeling of security. I know married women who do not feel secure because they do not have the complete love of their husbands. If you don't feel confident in his love for you, and/or in the commitment you've made with him, something will always be missing and you won't feel completely happy and fulfilled.

How to create this kind of love is largely what this book is about, but before we can even begin to discuss the principles involved in awakening true love, we need to see how *sex* affects relationships. If sex enters the relationship before a solid foundation of love has been established, then quite often you destroy your chances of ever building this kind of love. The only way your heart can truly open up and fully experience the joy and freedom that love offers is if you feel completely secure in your relationship. But to create the foundation of love, trust, and respect takes times and patience. It requires many hours of long

Love Before Sex

conversation and undergoing many different experiences together, without sex in the picture. The process may take several months before tender feelings of love have been established, or before you realize the two of you aren't a match.

If sex occurs before the foundation is built, you tend to lose your balance and become insecure. You lose control of your emotions, and your judgment is altered. It's much more difficult for you to assess him, your true feelings, and the possibility of a future together. But if you choose to *postpone* sex until you receive confirmation for yourself that you should continue in the relationship until love has been established, and until commitments have been made, then your relationship will be supported by a more solid foundation. You will be able to discern who he really is, what his true intentions are, and what you really feel about him. And you can do so without the uncertainty and fears that casual sex can create. You will still experience many emotions, and you can still be spontaneous in your relationships. But you won't experience the emptiness, the doubt, and the frustration that you typically feel when sex comes too soon.

CAROLYN

Carolyn was twenty-two when she met Ron.

"The first night Ron and I met we were in a club and we talked all evening. I gave him my number, and I believe we saw each other the next night or soon after that. After our first date, he invited me over to his place. I said no because I knew it was the 'right' answer since it was only our first date. I really liked him, so I didn't want to ruin it. He was a perfect gentleman. He didn't push me at all.

Chapter 1 Love Is The Goal

"The next time we went out, we stayed out very late and I had a lot to drink. Again he invited me over. This time I accepted. It's funny, but I actually felt okay about saying yes then, because after all, I had said no last time. It's as though in my mind, I thought I had resisted for a long time, even though it was only one date!

"From that moment on, we were what Ron called 'glued together.' We almost never left each other's side. That's partly why I didn't have a lot of remorse after becoming sexual with him so soon. I thought to myself, 'This is great! Finally a man who loves me no matter what and doesn't just leave me after he gets what he wants.'

"I moved in with him almost immediately. It seemed like we had been together for years, and yet we had only known each other for a few weeks. Living together seemed like the thing to do because, after all, we were together constantly, and Ron wasn't proposing marriage (there was no way *I* would make that suggestion). Also, we were in love—or so I thought.

"Ron could not or would not say I love you. I didn't want to say it until he did, but why wouldn't he ever say it? We were so intimate with one another, wasn't it only natural that we would verbally express our feelings? When I finally couldn't stand it any longer, I confronted Ron about his feelings. He told me he just couldn't say something if he didn't feel it. He cared for me and loved me as a person but that's as far as he could go. What a blow! Even though he did care for me, I thought we were in love. I thought that's what two people who were making love and living together were all about. I was wrong.

"The only thing I ever wanted in life was to be loved. I thought I finally had that, and now in one split second, it

Love Before Sex

all became a fantasy. It wasn't real. I cried and cried. I tried so hard to figure out what went wrong. But did I move out? Not until a year later. I was too afraid. Where would I go? I'd be all alone, with no one to be there for me. Even though he didn't love me, I felt I desperately loved him.

"Then it became my mission to win his love. It didn't matter that he wasn't right for me (something I discovered later). It only mattered that I turn the situation around. Ron was very good to me. He was generous financially. He showered me with gifts. He was fully committed to me in the sense that we were exclusive. We enjoyed many things together. Ron was also very complimentary and was always building me up to our friends. He was a *nice* guy. But I still felt like a guest in his house. It definitely wasn't *our* house. When I finally did bring up the subject of marriage, he said he just wasn't ready, or he wasn't interested in getting married, or that his finances weren't in order enough to get married.

"I thought things would change. But they didn't and I found myself becoming more and more bitter and angry. I thought, 'I'll show him! When I save enough money to leave, he'll be sorry!'

"The day came when I did leave, and he didn't stop me. He did express some sadness, but he didn't come after me with a marriage proposal. It took me a long time to get over that relationship."

What Carolyn Had

Carolyn had a relationship with a good man who grew to care for her. Yet, he didn't *cherish* her; his love was not deep and solid. Even though they agreed not to see other people, clearly something was missing. Ron wasn't willing to make any promises because he feelings hadn't been properly developed enough. They seemed to be just "playing house." Carolyn had a false sense of security. It appeared that she had it all—a nice home to live in and a kind man to share her life with. But she didn't have the things that mattered the most to her: true love and security.

The Problem

Carolyn approached this relationship in the best way she knew how at the time (remember, she was only twenty-two!). She honestly felt okay with the way things were progressing because they *were* progressing. After all, they went from dating to living together—that seemed like a major jump to her. Her self-esteem was such that as long as he showed continued interest, she was happy. She said no to sex on the first date because she knew it was the correct thing to do, not because of her true values and a clear understanding of how sex affects a relationship. She hadn't actually established her values yet, and she clearly had sex way too soon. When she met Ron, she could tell he was a good person, and they hit it off so well that she thought it felt right. But she didn't take the time to find out or discuss what Ron really wanted in a relationship, what his goals were, or how he truly felt about her. Carolyn found out far too late that Ron never truly loved her. That should never happen.

Moving in with him without further clarification of these points didn't help the situation. She still felt lonely and empty in the relationship. Carolyn didn't have the basic understanding of how to nurture the relationship and awaken deep feelings of love in her man. Therefore, Ron's feelings and level of commitment to her didn't develop properly. Perhaps they weren't meant to be

Love Before Sex

together, but that would have become obvious with time—before making the commitment of living together.

I should add here that there are many potential reasons why a woman might end up in a similar situation. She may have been very young and naïve at the time. Maybe she came from a dysfunctional background that seriously damaged her feelings of self-worth. Maybe she was just going through a bad time. Even more likely is that she honestly didn't know things would turn out this way. She had high hopes that it would lead to marriage. But the point is, she could have had more had she not jumped in to sex so soon—either Ron would have fallen deeply in love with her and they would have had a much better relationship, or they would have discovered that they weren't right for each other and not gotten involved in the first place.

TONYA

Tonya met James one year ago at a party. Within two months they had sex. Tonya said that they found themselves unable to hold back in the heat of the moment. The atmosphere that night had been very romantic, and they had plenty of chemistry. Even though they have been in a committed relationship for a year, the relationship isn't what Tonya had hoped for.

"James spends almost every night with me, although he keeps his own place. I've suggested that he give up his place and just move in, but he refuses. I love having him with me every night, but I hate the fact that we almost never go out. He says he's extremely busy with his career, which limits his free time. I usually end up spending the weekends alone or with girlfriends.

Chapter 1 Love Is The Goal

"I really love James, but he can make me crazy! He sometimes doesn't call when he says he will, he's often late, and he's not very affectionate when we are out in public together or around his friends. But what can I do?"

Despite having been together for a year, the topic of marriage has never come up. Tonya doesn't feel comfortable raising it because she doesn't want James to feel pressured. She knows that the mention of marriage might scare him away, and intuitively she realizes they aren't at that point yet. Tonya is very patient. She just takes it all in stride, hoping that in time things will change.

What Tonya Wants

Tonya wants to get married and have a family. She wants security and to know that her partner will be there for her forever.

What Tonya has

What Tonya wants, and what she is getting, are two very different things. Tonya thinks she has a relationship, but what she really has is a sexual partner who *at times* treats her with tenderness—which is what keeps her locked in. Most of the time, however, Tonya is neglected and mistreated; she finds herself lonely and frustrated. She doesn't have the sincere love of her man, even though he may be loyal to her.

The Problem

As usual, the problem began in the beginning of the relationship. Tonya and James became intimate in the heat of the moment, not because they consciously made a decision to be together in a monogamous relationship. They ended up being monogamous, but more out of convenience than

Love Before Sex

anything else. Neither of them had anyone else in their lives. They liked each other, and they had had sex. So being together was the obvious result. But it was less than adequate in Tonya's mind. *She had sex with James without any kind of discussion about where the relationship was going and what his intentions were.* Essentially, she agreed to enter into a "situation," where she had very few rights, without any solid hope for a future. Several months had passed before James felt the discussion of commitment was even appropriate, even though they were having sex. Tonya felt as though she gave a lot more than she received, and she was right. She gave far too much, too soon. Then, by continuing to give of herself, yet receive the treatment James gave her, her feelings of self-worth were seriously affected.

What Tonya Could Have Done

Tonya found herself in a sexual relationship with James because she didn't know what her standards (her sexual values) were from the beginning. It could be said that perhaps she didn't have any standards, but I believe she wasn't in touch with them. Tonya hadn't become clear on these issues yet, therefore she was more vulnerable to sexual advances.

It could also be said that Tonya knew her standards, but hey, she's only human. Romance and emotions aren't so logical and calculating! But the issue here is, *Tonya wants the kind of love described in this chapter. She wants marriage.* And she's dissatisfied with the status quo. And, as we'll continue to see, having sex blindly in this way and avoiding establishing a solid foundation, will not give her what she wants. Tonya needs to make the firm decision

Chapter 1 Love Is The Goal

that she won't have sex until she's in a committed, monogamous relationship with a man who loves her. And then she needs to stick to that, *no matter what.* Exactly how to accomplish this is what this book is all about.

THERESA

Theresa is involved with a married man. It wasn't that she wanted to get involved with him, it just happened.

"I was so tired of being alone. I've been single for many years and it isn't often that I meet someone I like. I just wanted to get close to a man. I wanted that male-female interaction. Along came Jedd. We sort of bumped into each other, and we developed a great friendship. You never plan these things, and of course, I resisted any of kind of involvement because of his marriage. But how could I resist for long? He was so warm, nurturing, funny, sensitive, and extremely sexy. We began having a sexual relationship after a couple of months. Now he comes over when he can. I know he's not going to leave his wife for me, but right now I don't care. I just love the intimacy we share when we are together. He says things that really show he cares. He tells me how much he enjoys seeing me and how he misses me when we're not together."

What Theresa Wants

When I asked Theresa what she ultimately wants, she said marriage. She told me how hard it is to accept Jedd leaving on vacations with his family. *She* wants to be the one who plans a vacation with her own husband. She wants to share her life with someone on a daily basis, not just whenever he can get away for a moment, primarily for sex.

What Theresa Has

It's pretty clear that Theresa has a "situation" based on sex. They have other interests, and they do enjoy a certain amount of companionship, but even Theresa admitted that it's the sex that keeps him coming back. They don't go out, which really hurts Theresa. But she doesn't want to lose what she considers intimacy. She allowed herself to get sucked in to a situation that brings her more unhappiness and frustration than joy and fulfillment, and yet all she can see are the loving, tender moments, because she is so starved for them.

The Problem

Theresa is in denial. She thinks she's getting enough of her needs to make it worth it, but she admits profound frustration. She is clearly settling for much less than what is possible for her. Yet, she doesn't see it that way. She has told me many times that although she may not be getting the relationship she has always wanted, she does have a lot more than what she has had for many years. She wants to be loved, and this is the closest thing she can find for now—but settling for this relationship may be preventing her from meeting a man who is available to really love her.

Whereas Theresa used to want love and marriage for herself, she has now become obsessed with simply having satisfying times together with Jedd. Her focus is now on when he will call or if he will call. It isn't even about finding a man for herself anymore. Jedd gives her just enough to keep her hooked.

Theresa convinces herself that it's better than nothing. But when she describes what it's like in between the times she sees Jedd, it's no picnic. She's elated when she sees him, but when he leaves, a pattern begins to emerge. She waits for him to call. He never seems to call when she wants him to or expects him to. Then she's full of despair. She feels depressed and hurt. She begins to pull herself out of it and then she starts to become strong. She convinces herself that it doesn't matter and that she doesn't need him. She tells herself that she's not in love with him. Just when she becomes okay with the whole situation and regains her strength, he calls. She's drawn back into the entire cycle all over again.

What Theresa Could Have Done

The solution lies in Theresa rebuilding her self-esteem in order to feel worthy of true love, and then vow to never settle for anything less than the real deal. She honestly doesn't believe she's worthy of a real relationship. She doesn't believe it can or will happen for her. Rather than finding ways to get what she wants, she settles for so much less. She knew what she was getting into with Jedd, but she didn't know how to prevent herself from getting involved with him because she wasn't strong enough emotionally. Essentially, she rationalized and justified a very destructive situation. What she needed to do was stay as far away from Jedd as possible the minute she realized what he wanted. The answer is always *no* to married men. Period. Actually, from now on, the answer is no to any men who are not worthy and/or who are emotionally unavailable.

As Theresa directs her attention to rebuilding her self-esteem and making room for a healthy relationship, she can break the pattern.

Although each of these stories are very different, there are some clear similarities. All three women desperately want to be in a relationship. Yet, their desire to connect with someone overpowers everything else.

Two out of the three women expressed that they knew they were with the wrong person. It wasn't so much that they were only together for sex, but sex artificially prolonged these otherwise doomed relationships.

Tonya may have been able to develop a beautiful, solid relationship with James had she set a different standard in the beginning, but because a solid base wasn't established *first*; the relationship never seemed to be completely right.

All three women suffer from low self-esteem, which is apparent simply because they didn't ensure that their own needs were met and they allowed the men to treat them poorly. The saddest part of all is that all of these women yearned for love, yet none of them had it.

> *By saying no to sex without commitment and love, you are creating the opportunity for men to seriously consider what their true feelings for you are. They actually have to take notice and think about their intentions because they know casual sex isn't a possibility.*

The One-Night Stand, Few-Weeks Stand, and Few-Months Stand

We are all familiar with the one-night stand. But how is it different when sex occurs very early on and then the relationship lasts a few days, weeks, or even months?

If sex occurred within the first few dates, chances are it won't be a life-long love affair that everyone raves about. You have to ask yourself what it is you really want. It may not have been a "one-night stand", but if it lasted a few weeks it's basically the same thing, it just lasted a little longer.

Even couples who have been together for years can suffer stagnation of their relationship because they had sex too soon in the beginning of their relationship. These are the kinds of involvements that you need to avoid if you ever hope to build true love that lasts.

The Emotional Pain Sex Can Cause

Nothing is more painful than allowing yourself to be sexually vulnerable with a man, only to have his feelings and behavior change. Even worse is not hearing form him for days, weeks, months, or ever again. It's humiliating, degrading, embarrassing, and very hurtful. Yet women sometimes make the same mistake over and over again. They crave love and closeness. They allow their hormones to get the best of them. They become seduced by a smooth talker who convinces them that they have more of a relationship than they really do. Maybe you have vowed to never do it again, but you still don't have a plan for how to handle the next situation. You still don't know how long you should wait, and you don't know what to do in the meantime.

Let me reassure you that you never have to feel that pain again. You never have to experience the heartache and remorse that casual sex creates. If this has been a pattern for you, then it's time for you to be excited about your future because by the time you finish reading this book, you will be equipped with the techniques and strategies necessary to break this pattern. Don't give up hope. You have the power to change and to create the life you've always wanted.

> *Women are not necessarily less sexual than men. But sex affects women differently. Women are more vulnerable than men when it comes to sex. That's why women need to protect their hearts and bodies. Someone has to ensure that love and commitment are present before having sex. If there are men who share this standard for themselves, great. But women's greater vulnerability means they need to make their own decisions independently.*

Do You Need this Message?

If you're wondering whether or not this message will apply to you personally, ask yourself the following questions and see if they apply to you now, or if they have applied in the past.

- Do you often doubt his love for you?
- Do you feel you give so much more?
- Do you often feel taken for granted?
- Do you feel that he maintains you as a sex object rather than a potential lifetime mate?
- Does he resist committing to you even though you are having sex?
- Is he unwilling to marry you even though you have been together a substantial period of time?
- Does he resist saying, "I love you" even though you have been in a sexual relationship for awhile?

Chapter 1 Love Is The Goal

- Does he say "I love you" strictly as a means of holding onto you?
- Do you find yourself feeling angry and resentful toward him or men in general? Are you sick of living like a gypsy, staying at his place then yours?
- Do you sometimes feel lonely even though you are in a relationship?
- Do you sometimes feel that it's the sex that keeps you together?

If you find yourself nodding yes to one or more of these questions, you're settling for a lot less than what is really possible for you. In each case, the cart is before the horse. The attachment is to sex, not love. By acknowledging the truth in your own relationship, you make a start to change. You have to know that what you have is not necessarily what you want. And you have to believe that you do deserve more. None of us has to settle for less than the highest form of love.

Do You Lead with Your Sexuality?

Ask yourself the following questions to determine if sex is more of a priority in your life than you might realize:

- Do you consciously or unconsciously believe that all you primarily have to offer is your sexuality?
- Do you believe that it is through hot sex that you get a man?
- Do you use sex as an escape? Is it more like an addiction for you?
- Do you lack the confidence to say no to sex?
- Do you believe that he'll lose interest in you if you don't have sex?
- Do you have to have a few drinks before you have sex?

19

Love Before Sex

- Do you believe that you have to offer up kinky, wild sex in order to sustain his interest?
- Do you dress provocatively as a way to draw men to you?
- Do you see men's sexual attention toward you as positive attention?

If you answered yes to any of these questions then you have some healing to do. It's important to get to a place where you:

1) acknowledge your worth
2) accept the past and embrace it as part of you
3) make a decision to heal and overcome your challenges with the help of a professional
4) complete a sexual history chart (see chapter 11)
5) eliminate all negative/sexually-based relationships in your life
6) outline your goals

These are just a few things you can do to get on track. Most importantly, realize that you never have to lead with your sexuality. That never gets you love, only sex.

Do You Find Yourself in "Situations" Rather Than in Relationships?

If your involvement is based on sex, it is quite often more like a "situation" than a real relationship. It's easy to tell if it's a situation. All you have to do is ask yourself the following questions (in addition to the ones you just read):

- Are you embarrassed at all about your involvement with this person?
- Do you keep it a secret from your friends and family, possibly only telling a best friend?

- Do you know there is absolutely no future with this person yet remain out of convenience or what you may be getting out of it (which could be strictly sex, financial security, companionship, and protection)?
- Do you know deep down inside that there is something "not right" about the situation?
- Do you know intuitively that this person is somehow "beneath you"?
- Is he involved with another woman (either married, seeing someone else, just getting out of a relationship, or still hung up on someone)?

If you answered yes to any of these questions, you may have a pattern of getting stuck in situations rather than building real relationships. A therapist or Life Coach can sometimes help us determine why we create these patterns in our lives. You want to quickly get into the solution and become available for a real and meaningful relationship. It doesn't have to take years—you can do the work and overcome your challenges in a time frame that makes sense. All that is required to begin is a *decision*. Of course, you can't make a decision to change a pattern if you aren't even aware of the pattern. But once you've gained the self-awareness, all it takes is a commitment to change. It isn't easy, but it is possible. You don't have to be a victim of your past forever.

The following vignettes are from interviews I conducted with women to illustrate their feelings about sex and what it means to them. You may not relate to all of them, but you can learn from each of their experiences:

MADISON, 38

I didn't lose my virginity until I was nineteen. I was known as a "good girl." Then I went off to college and slept with several men, one after another. I was out of my normal surroundings, so I guess I was more vulnerable. I confused sex with love. I wanted love, yet I didn't. I was scared to death of it. I slept with so many sleazy guys, all of whom didn't want a relationship either. I didn't feel good about myself to begin with, so sleeping with a bunch of losers proved what a nothing I was. I could say, "See, I am a loser!" Even the *losers* don't want me!

SHARLA, 48

Sex has always been a way for me to get what I want. I thought because of my good looks and sexy body, I could pretty much manipulate any man into giving me what I want. I ask myself all the time, *"What was I doing?"* I ruined my life in a way and for what? Some attention? A good time? Gifts, money, trips? All I ever really wanted was love. But my pride wouldn't allow me to admit that. Deep down, I longed for a family of my own, just like my sister has. I often watch her with envy. She seems to have everything I've ever wanted. Her husband adores her. They take care of each other. Sex is just a part of their relationship. I guess I never truly believed I could have something that good. I had sex for all the wrong reasons. It had nothing to do with love, it was only a tool.

CHELSEA, 33

I've never actually thought about what sex means to me—not in any detail, that is. I've just accepted the fact that it's part of a relationship. It's just something that happens when the time seems right. Now I'm re-evaluating if this is smart. I have to admit, I don't want to continue having sex with several more partners. I'd like to settle down with just one man.

LEAH, 50

I know this may sound crazy, but I find myself getting sexually involved with men I would never consider marrying. That seems safer to me. If I were to meet someone with real potential, then I'd try very hard to do everything right. But I haven't had much luck with that. It seems like it's always the *next* woman these men end up marrying.

Is a Good Relationship Possible if You Have Sex Too Soon?

A relationship is not necessarily doomed just because you have sex too soon. Relationships are complicated and there are many reasons why they don't work out. You may simply not be right for each other, or he turned out to be a jerk, or the timing was off... but I promise you, if you do the exercises in this book and read with an open mind, you will discover that if you trace your relationships back to the beginning, that sex too soon was the primary culprit for the demise of the relationship. There may be plenty of other reasons, or excuses if you will, but had you not had sex so soon and instead followed the guidelines in this book, I guarantee that you would have had a very different result.

Sometimes relationships work out despite having sex too soon. Stewart, 37, and Gina, 35, are a perfect example of this. They fell in love almost immediately. Stewart knew very quickly that Gina was the woman for him, and even after they had sex, he felt the same way. They were together constantly from that day forward. There was no formal discussion of commitment or love. They even ended up getting married.

Camille, 29, and Kevin, 32, dated for a couple of weeks and had sex without having a prior discussion. Today they have a great relationship. They really seem to love each other.

So how did these two couples succeed when so many others fail? In these cases, both couples were very much in love *before they ever became physical.* They each knew it was more than just a passing fancy. They just failed to verbalize their feelings before they had sex. Sometimes two people meet and it's almost like destiny. They know they are meant to be together. They both feel secure in the other's feelings.

The question is, how often does this happen? How often have you felt he was your destiny only to discover that he's now part of your history? It's a huge risk to take, especially considering that this is one of the most important decisions of your life. The problem is, when it's new, it's common to feel as if "this could be it". And the guy is often extremely attentive and some men really lay it on thick in the beginning (sometimes only as an attempt to get into your pants). But that doesn't necessarily mean it is true love. If you feel that strongly about each other, then it won't hurt to at least discuss the future and his intentions.

Chapter 1 Love Is The Goal

Separating Fiction from Fact

False Assumptions:

- *If you become intimate, he will feel committed to you.*
- *Sex has to be a part of every relationship—it's just the way it is.*
- *You have to be sexy to get a man.*
- *Once you have sex, it's automatically a relationship.*
- *If the sex is great, he will never leave you.*
- *You will get a man to love you because he will become so dependent upon the sex.*
- *Most men aren't willing to have a relationship without sex.*
- *Sex is just a physical experience—there are no emotional elements.*

The Truth:

- *Sex has nothing to do with getting a commitment or gaining a husband.*
- *Without at least a verbal commitment to be exclusive, you have nothing concrete.*
- *Great sex may keep him there for a time, but it's not as important to him as you think. It won't necessarily keep him interested in you.*
- *Sex does not have to be a part of every relationship. You do have a choice.*
- *Sex (especially if it occurs too soon) is not what will make a relationship great, lasting, or loving.*
- *Sex does not affect men in the same way that it does women.*

The Sweet Rewards

Putting love before sex offers many rewards. These points will be discussed in greater detail throughout the next couple of chapters, but here is an outline of the benefits of waiting until love and commitment has been established (or engagement, or marriage, whichever you prefer). As you read through this list, imagine what it would be like to experience these feelings consistently.

You Will Create a Place for True Love to Grow

- The two of you will not be preoccupied with sex.
- The relationship will not be sabotaged by having sex too soon.
- It will be easier to determine true feelings and eliminate much of the confusion sex can create.
- Your relationship will be based on love, respect, commitment, and trust.

You Will be Protected

- You will be able to determine what his true intentions are and you will weed out the men who aren't serious.
- You won't be overly vulnerable too early in the relationship. You will feel secure.

Your Self-Esteem Will Grow

- You will gain self-respect.
- You will gain peace of mind.
- You won't feel like a sex object or that your relationship is based on sex.
- You will be in control of your relationship.
- You will experience freedom from within.

- You will feel good about yourself and experience more confidence than ever before.
- You will be free from guilt and fear.
- You will feel good about being true to yourself (and to your religious/spiritual beliefs, if they coincide).

You Will be More Attractive to Men

- You will stand out as unique and special.
- You will be seen as a disciplined, thoughtful woman.
- You will gain tremendous respect.
- You will be seen as someone who cares about herself physically, emotionally, and spiritually.
- You will be more radiant as a result of gaining peace of mind and happiness.

Note: There are obvious dangers with having sex at all, such as sexually transmitted diseases. If you are going to have sex, protect yourself by having "safer" sex. Only abstinence is completely safe, but using condoms can reduce the physical risks.

> *Waiting to have sex doesn't necessarily guarantee that true love will grow. Sometimes, no matter what you do, a particular relationship is not going to work, even if you do obtain a commitment, or even get married. Waiting does, however, create an opportunity for true love to grow.*

Chapter 2
How Sex Before Love Sabotages True Love

You've met someone new, and you're crazy about him. The minute the two of you met, you knew this was going to be something big. The first night you went out, you talked until two in the morning. He gave you a tender kiss on the cheek as he said good-night. You couldn't sleep, you could think only of him. He called the next day to tell you what a great time he had and now he couldn't wait to see you again. You saw each other several times over the next week, each date more incredible than the last. You talked about the future and what both of you want in life. He said he had never met a woman as special as you.

Finally, you are both alone in his apartment and you're kissing. One thing leads to another, and you end up having sex. The next morning as you are getting ready to leave, he says, "I'll call you." You kiss each other good-bye, and the rest of the day you are on cloud nine. You can't stop thinking about him, reflecting on the night before. As evening approaches, he still hasn't called. You make sure you don't wander too far from the phone so you are sure to get his call. It gets later and later. You feel a little hurt. You go to bed thinking he must have been busy. Oh well, you assure yourself, he'll call tomorrow. But tomorrow comes and goes, still with no phone call. Now your stomach begins to knot. You feel more and more depressed. You wonder what he is doing and why he hasn't called. You are now unable to focus on your work or enjoy anything you do. You feel sick about the whole thing and wish you hadn't slept with him.

Maybe this man does call after three or four days have passed, or maybe he doesn't call at all. Either way, it can be devastating for a woman. Women typically feel that by having sex the relationship automatically moves to a new level and that if they feel more emotionally attached to him, he must feel the same way. So when he doesn't call, you get the message that you weren't that special after all. You feel deeply hurt and rightly so—you shared a very personal and intimate part of yourself with someone you trusted. You trusted that he cared about you, and that he felt the same way you did. The problem is, when you have sex too soon, it rarely if ever progresses the way you want it to. Sex too soon simply changes everything.

SEX CHANGES EVERYTHING

Sex radically changes a relationship because of the profound emotional effect it has on women. The problem is that many people—men and women alike—want to ignore this fact. They want to pretend that both sexes can simply enjoy sex without any ties as a purely physical pleasure. In truth, we just aren't set up that way as human beings. Sex affects men and women differently. Although there are exceptions, women need to stop pretending that they are emotionally invincible when it comes to sex. Because women become emotionally bonded through sex, they have to take greater precautions to protect themselves. If you didn't bond emotionally, you wouldn't feel used or taken for granted if things didn't work out. Belinda, 53, said, "Every man I have ever been with has made it very clear that if I wanted to use them for sex, to go right ahead. They seem to have no problem with the idea of having sex without any ties." Esther, 46, said, "Most men do not see a direct correlation between sex and love. They seem to be able to have relationships that are based strictly on sex. It's almost as though they know women who they might consider just for sex and women they would consider for a serious relationship."

I'm not saying that all men are uncaring, sex-crazed animals. However, we have to be honest and face the difference between the sexes. Adele, 36, said, "I have never known a man who wasn't willing to have sex with me if I gave them the green light. As long as I'm game, so are they." Martina, 40, said, Men want sex, that's all there is to it. Maybe that isn't all they want, but if they have an opportunity to have sex with a woman, they are going to do it. They don't think in terms of emotional attachment." There are many men who may be offended by these remarks, but even men who don't think this way acknowledge that they know plenty of men who do. It's a fact of life.

Many men are unaware of these differences and that's partly because women haven't acknowledged them as well. Even though they may have experienced this difference in men's and women's reactions several times, men usually don't understand why it's happening. They only know women usually freak out at a certain point in the relationship, become more possessive, and want more of a commitment. They may not consider that the reason women behave so differently after sex is because of a chemical reaction.

OXYTOCIN

Oxytocin is a chemical that is released when you have sex, affecting the neurotransmitters in your brain. It's sometimes called "the bonding hormone" because it causes you to have warm fuzzies for the person with whom you're sexually active. I first learned of Oxytocin through Dr. Pat Allen, author of *"Getting to I Do."* As I continued researching the phenomenon, I found that this is the same chemical that is released when a mother gives birth and nurses, which causes her to feel the overwhelming desire to coddle her baby and it creates a deep emotional bond with the child. Men have the same chemical released during sex but not nearly to the same degree, which means most men do not become as bonded. This explains so much! It explains why men can have casual sex and it means nothing. It explains why women can have sex with someone they barely like, only to be waiting by the phone for his call after sex. Oxytocin forces you to see him differently after sex. You want to cuddle and spend more time together, and naturally you want to become more serious, whereas he is looking for the door (if he doesn't love you).

Megan, 24, dated a man to whom she really had not been attracted. Somehow they ended up having sex, and once they did, he amazingly transformed before her eyes. He became her Adonis. She felt jealous if he went out with anyone else, waited for his calls, and broke plans with her friends to be with him. Yet, this was a guy she earlier had not even been interested in!

Chapter 2 How Sex Before Love Sabotages True Love

Knowing that Oxytocin affects you in this way should create a big shift within you. We aren't dealing with an even playing field—Oxytocin makes us different, and therefore we have to approach the relationship, specifically the sexual aspect of the relationship, differently. Because Oxytocin runs a number on your emotions you have to be extra cautious and not allow it to have its effect before he loves you.

DONNA

"I had just separated from my husband and my self-esteem was at a low point. I was so miserable I didn't want to get out of bed in the morning. I wondered if I ever would be in a relationship again. Then one day I met my new neighbor, Stan. He was really nice and easy to talk to. We became friends and began spending a lot of time together. We went to the movies and out to dinner. He called me almost every day. We developed a wonderful friendship in four months.

"I knew the relationship probably wouldn't go anywhere ultimately, and I was not in love. But I felt so needy at the time; I wanted intimacy. We became particularly close one night and Stan said, 'Are you sure you want to do this because I just don't know if we should.' All I could say was, 'Yes! We *should* do it! I *want* to!' And we did. I had no idea I was going to fall so head over heels in love with him. I just didn't plan on that happening. I thought I could remain in control. But I fell hard.

"I guess Stan could tell how strongly I felt and it scared him. We still spent time together, but I could feel him pulling back. He didn't want to take me to a Christmas party he had been invited to because he said he wanted to go alone and

33

maybe even meet other women. He said he didn't want to be a 'couple'. He even said, 'Donna, we're not an *item!*' That really hurt, especially after all the physical closeness we had shared. He made it clear that he wanted space and that he didn't want the pressure or responsibility of a serious relationship.

"So we stopped having sex, and although we have remained friends, there seems to be no chance for a romantic involvement. It's very painful, but there is nothing I can do. I'm tired of trying to figure out what went wrong and why Stan didn't fall in love with me."

This is a story I hear often. What stands out for me is that Donna, and so many women like her, settle for so much less than what they can have and what they deserve. Even though Donna told me that she bonded emotionally with every man she had been with before, it didn't enter her mind that the same thing might happen this time. She assumed it was okay to have sex because of how well the two of them had hit it off, and she didn't think she ultimately wanted Stan anyway. She also was so emotionally off-kilter at the time that her mind wasn't clear. Also, the fact that they waited such a long time (4 months is a very long time these days!) made her feel even more secure. She didn't think it was necessary to talk about commitment. But Stan and Donna were a long way from being in love. They really liked each other. They were friends. But that was it.

When I asked Donna if she felt the relationship with Stan would have turned out differently had they discussed issues such as where the relationship was going, their feelings, and commitment, she said, "If we had discussed all of those issues, then we would not have had sex." And if they

Chapter 2 How Sex Before Love Sabotages True Love

hadn't had sex, Donna wouldn't have bonded emotionally, which led to her coming on so strong—which caused Stan to pull away. They would have continued to build a friendship (which would have been nice to have during the difficult time Donna was going through). Maybe they would have fallen in love—or maybe they would have simply remained friends. But Donna wouldn't be devastated and in so much pain. She was embarrassed, humiliated, hurt, angry, and confused. It was the last thing she needed, given the state she was already in from her divorce.

Stan and Donna knew the answers to these questions before they had sex, they just didn't verbalize them. Neither of them were making any commitments and neither really wanted to. Which would have been fine for Donna—except that she became emotionally bonded as a result of having sex (Oxytocin), and therefore her feelings changed. She was the one who lost out in the end. Stan said that hurting her was the last thing he wanted to do, but he was not feeling more connected to her (less Oxytocin and he wasn't in love before having sex).

"I knew when I was having sex with him that I was taking a big risk, but I didn't care at the time. I was so lonesome. I had felt so rejected by my ex-husband that it just felt good to have someone else show that much interest in me. I was feeling ugly and old and I wondered if anyone would ever love me. And there was this nice guy who wanted to be with me."

Donna began to see that although she thought she was getting her needs met, she really was denying them and setting herself up for more heartache. Her true needs never were met—what she got was a temporary fix and more pain, as a result of settling for sex versus holding out for love.

JANE

Once I was very lonely on a New Year's Eve. I went to a local hang-out place and I ran into a guy I had seen before. We had sex right away. I asked him what his ideal woman was. He told me she had a face like Heather Locklear, a body like Dolly Parton, and a personality like Donna Reed. Well, here I was—my hair was bright red at the time, I was wearing black leather, I was an angry feminist (nothing like Donna Reed) and I was skinny (nothing like Dolly, that's for sure!). We were having a sexual relationship, and yet we didn't know each other. We were obviously not right for each other. I just figured, 'Oh well, it's too late. We are on this course now. We're a couple.' Since we were a couple, I began expecting certain things, like spending a certain amount of time together. I felt this bond, like I should be setting up house with him, but I didn't even like the guy! That's how sex affects me. I feel a bond, even when I don't want to. Our relationship wasn't tender, the sex was not like *making love*, and it was just something we did.

"I couldn't picture myself taking him home to Mom and Dad, and I couldn't picture him being my husband. That's the most frustrating part—you get attached to him, and there is nowhere to put him! You can't plan a life together, so you are in a perpetual state of limbo. He eventually dumped me, which now that I look back I'm grateful for, because I just couldn't end these relationships. I felt too powerless.

"You can't ask for anything more because he has nothing to give, and you don't feel it is your right anyway. It's just a horrible place to be. I know a lot of women get very angry when men don't give of themselves financially, when they don't feel any sense of responsibility to them even though they are sexual together. But why should they? Men do not *owe* us anything. It's up to us to make sure our needs will be met before we get too involved with a man. The promise is equal—when we marry, we commit to being there for him also."

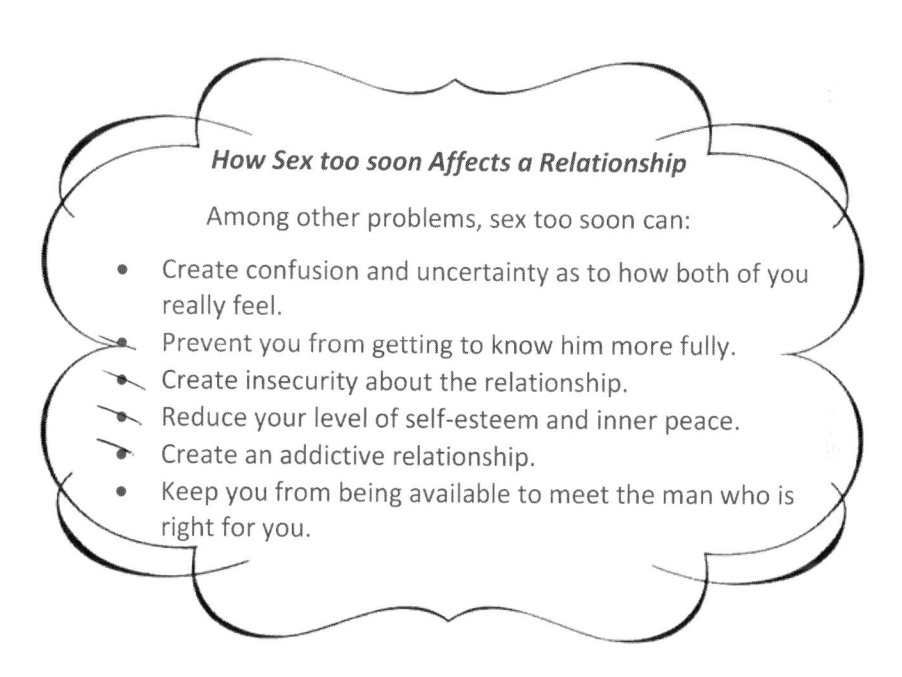

> **How Sex too soon Affects a Relationship**
>
> Among other problems, sex too soon can:
>
> - Create confusion and uncertainty as to how both of you really feel.
> - Prevent you from getting to know him more fully.
> - Create insecurity about the relationship.
> - Reduce your level of self-esteem and inner peace.
> - Create an addictive relationship.
> - Keep you from being available to meet the man who is right for you.

3 EXCEPTIONS TO THE BONDING RULE

There are a few times when certain women seem to be able to have sex with men and not bond emotionally.

1) **Women who seem to respond more like men.** These women usually have a strong masculine energy,

even though they may also be quite feminine. Perhaps they have higher testosterone levels than most women. They seem to be able to have sex without getting emotionally attached, just as most men are able to do. Quite often, these women are the sexual aggressors. They may have one or more lovers without any commitments and appear to be unfazed by it all. I see this more and more with women all the time. However, even some of these women who seem so self-contained and invincible have been known to break down and tearfully express the pain they experience in relationships. They want to be loved and cherished just as much as other woman.

Very few women are able to have casual sex for long without experiencing painful repercussions. Many women start out thinking they can handle it, only to find out they can't. Or, they think they can change the man's feelings. Lila, 29, put it this way: "When Jake told me he wasn't ready for a serious relationship, I figured I could change his mind. I wasn't all that concerned when we had sex because I thought it would turn him around. But it didn't." Despite this, there are a few women who can emotionally handle having casual sex, and it is possible. The question is, Is it right for *you*?

2) **When the sex is not satisfying.** There is a notion that if he can satisfy you, he can have you. If not, it is difficult to get you to surrender. Men instinctively know this, which is why they try so hard to not only have sex with you, but to also please you sexually. It's not just for their egos—it's so they can win your heart and gain your devotion. They know if they cannot *move* you, you are going to be unimpressed. So, when the experience is less than adequate, it's fairly easy to

walk away without any problem—in fact, you usually can't wait to get away.

3) ***If you have had sex with him long before and you now reunite.*** You may have bonded the first time years ago, but the relationship didn't work out. Over time, the emotional bond you once had diminishes, at least partially. Then, you got back together and had sex. It just wasn't the same. Your feelings for him were not the same, and the entire experience just didn't work for you.

SEXUALLY AGGRESSIVE WOMEN

I'm pretty stunned at how aggressive women are today, especially the young women and even girls in high school and college. They are the ones who are making all the moves these days, without giving it a thought. Let's look at some of the comments of the *men* I interviewed:

JARED

"I dated a woman who insisted on having sex fairly early in the relationship. She convinced me that it was okay, but I told her I wasn't sure I was ready. I suggested that we get to know each other better first because sex does change everything. But she really wanted to have sex. I guess I could have put my foot down, but there we were in bed, naked, with the knowledge that if I didn't do it, I would be considered the biggest wimp of all time. The next day I felt weird about the whole thing. I could tell she was feeling closer to me, but I was feeling more and more clear that the relationship was not going to work out."

It is interesting to see that Jared actually warned this woman of his feelings, yet she ignored his words and chose to go ahead anyway. Maybe she thought she could change his mind, or that the sex would be so fantastic that he wouldn't want to leave. Either way, she is the one who ended up hurt. I asked Jared to further explain why he chose to have sex anyway, considering the doubts he had, and he said, "I didn't know I was going to feel that way the next day. I was attracted to her, and I wanted a relationship, so when she convinced me to go forward with sex, I thought maybe it would work."

The take-away message here is that when a guy tells you he's not ready, *listen to him!* Just as you want men to listen to you and honor your feelings, men deserve the same respect. Don't just aggressively move forward despite warnings, misgivings, and doubts. You want to really hear what the other person is saying (which may not always be so direct), and you want to make a joint decision about going forward sexually. There should be *no coercion*, on either side.

JOHN

"I have had a few relationships where we had sex without any commitment and after awhile we parted as friends without any bad feelings. But that has been a very small percentage compared to the number of relationships that ended badly because the women wanted more after having sex. I have learned that if I have sex with women who are not right for me, they usually become much more serious after sex, and I feel less serious about them. I withdraw, and they're hurt. I don't know why this happens, it just does. It's a pattern I have become aware of recently, but for years I was clueless. With one woman, I was concerned she was going to kill herself, she was in so much pain. But

Chapter 2 How Sex Before Love Sabotages True Love

the interesting thing is, with almost all of these relationships, I was totally honest with these women. I told them I was very attracted to them, but that I did not love them. I made it clear that if they were just interested in a casual relationship, I was game. They all said yes, they wanted to get involved, and they too were fine with a casual relationship. But it never worked out that way. They became much more emotionally attached. So I learned that to get someone to sign on the dotted line is not enough because feelings can change. It's amazing though, that these women seemed to want to have sex more than I did. In most cases, they were the aggressors."

Again, these women had no regard for his feelings, nor did they seem to care about their own. They possibly weren't aware of Oxytocin and its effects, but even if they did know that they become emotionally attached, they didn't seem to care. This means that self-control and delaying gratification weren't part of the game plan. *Self-gratification* and *instant* gratification was the name of the game! I wonder how these women felt about the situation a few weeks later, or however long it took, when things started to fall apart and the reality that John didn't love them and never would, set in.

JACK

Zara, 51, came on strong with Jack, 60. It was only their first date when she invited Jack up to her place for a night cap. She immediately started making out with Jack, much to his surprise. At a certain point she stopped him and said, "I think you better go." Now the foundation was set for more making out. That's what both of them were thinking about and their second date was more of the same, except that they went further, of course. This time

Love Before Sex

Zara gave Jack oral sex and they made out some more. She had the sense to explain to Jack that she "gets emotionally involved if she has sex", (that wasn't enough—she needed to talk about a lot more than that). Jack agreed that he too gets emotionally involved and so they decided to hold off on going forward sexually. However, it isn't surprising that they ended up having sex shortly thereafter, despite their intentions to take it slow and put sex off for awhile.

My experience has been that once the ball gets rolling in this direction, it continues all the way to the end very quickly. It's very difficult to stop the process. That's why it's better to not allow it to go there in the first place. Also, Zara has no idea what is going on in Jack's life. She doesn't even know him because it's only been one date! As it turns out, Jack just got out of a very painful relationship in which he was cheated on. He is definitely on the rebound and not ready for a serious involvement at this time. He wouldn't be a good candidate for a relationship and yet she didn't take the time to get to know anything about him. She just jumped in and made the moves, without considering that maybe it wasn't the best direction for her or him to go. And Jack should have put the brakes on, but he said, "I don't think she would have taken no for an answer!" When a woman comes on this strong, it's difficult for a man to stop the process. It's possible, but not probable.

The take-away message with this one is, ladies, take your time and get to know what is really going on with the man you're on the date with! It could be that he is still hooked on someone else, or he's nursing a broken heart, or he isn't even capable of loving someone—you simply don't know what you're dealing with on the first few dates.

So stop being sexually aggressive and put your energies into getting to know who he is and what his current situation is (without grilling him).

WHY SEX TOO SOON SCARES MEN AWAY

There are many reasons why sex affects men differently than it does women. We have already talked about Oxytocin. Here are a few more reasons why men sometimes get scared away after having sex.

Women's Expectations.

As you bond with a man, you begin to have certain expectations—all of which are perfectly natural, but that freak him out a bit. You expect him, for example, to have certain feelings for you. You either believe he loves you, or you think he should. You figure there should be a future together—after all, you just made love, didn't you? You expect him to treat you with more tenderness, more love, and more concern. You expect him to call you consistently and include you more fully in his life.

These are pretty heavy-duty expectations for a man, even though they seem perfectly reasonable to us. It is difficult for many men to sacrifice freedom and commit to one woman. The only thing that can get him to do so completely is a deep feeling of love for the woman. So you can imagine how utterly frightening it would be for a man to have these expectations placed upon him when he hasn't yet developed a strong love for the woman (and how can he develop deep feelings for her when he just met her?!). Quite often he just wants to get away. And even if you don't actually verbalize these expectations, men can feel them. They can see it in your eyes, and the way you react to them. If you don't have sex, however, you don't project expectations, and you are able to give him the space he needs to fall for you.

The Challenge is Gone

We all appreciate a challenge. If we get involved with someone who so easily gives of themselves without some sort of challenge, we don't appreciate it as much. We may not like that fact, but it is the nature of all human beings. As Thomas Paine once said, "What we obtain too cheap, we esteem too lightly; 'tis dearness only that gives everything its value."

It isn't that you are trying to be a challenge for its own sake. What you are doing is taking care of yourself and setting a higher standard. As a result of that, you naturally become more challenging to him.

Why would you want to do something that may clearly cause him to lose interest? Men would not think of buying a woman a diamond ring on the first date because it would be inappropriate. They may *feel* like doing it, but common sense tells them to hold back. In the very early stages of a relationship, both sides have to be very careful not to scare the other away by either wearing their heart on their sleeve or coming on too strong. Once love has been established and verbalized, both parties can be more free and just enjoy the relationship.

His Feelings for You Change

When a man can have you sexually without love or any other requirement, his feelings for you usually will change. Whereas in the beginning he may have felt intrigued and highly interested, if sex occurs before deeper feelings develop, he will typically begin to doubt his original feelings. All of the potential that was once there has dissipated, unfortunately.

What men tell me more than anything else is, if it was so easy for them to become sexual with a woman, then maybe it has been that way with other men. Men place a value on everything. If you are so easily attainable, they figure you are not worth as much as if they had to jump through some hoops to get you. This is another reason why you absolutely want to establish deep, loving feelings, including trust and respect—before you allow sex to become part of the relationship.

Men are Not the Problem

It is easy to blame men. "He lied to me!" "He led me on to believe there was more!" "He told me he loved me!" It's easy to feel like a victim. You were sucked in by a real Casanova, and once he got what he wanted, everything changed. Therefore, it's his fault. How could it not be? *He* was the one who came on so strong in the beginning and made all those promises. What could you have possibly done, except for maybe being stupid enough to fall for it?

Of course, some men will make promises they will not keep and some will have incredible integrity. But this is about *you* and *your* life. The best thing you can do is take full responsibility for yourself from now on, and not only watch for the red flags and don't have sex too soon—but don't allow anyone to take advantage of you again. Don't allow yourself to be duped by a smooth talker. Do you want to be a victim forever? Or do you want to take control of your destiny regardless of what others do? Also, as I pointed out earlier, it's quite often the women who are making all the moves today... so in that case you have only yourself to blame.

Why Love Must Come First

Men sometimes feel as though they are backed into a wall against their will. They feel more responsible as a result of having sex, and yet they don't want that responsibility. If they were in love, it would be okay because they already would have wrestled with the idea in their heads and made a decision to be committed. Then they would willingly take on the responsibility. "What responsibility?" You ask. A relationship is a big responsibility for both parties, but men see it as a huge commitment of their time, attention, money, and emotions. They don't give those things up easily (nor should you!). Only a deep, solid feeling of love will persuade him to commit. In fact, once a man falls in love, he will *want* to make sacrifices.

7 Pitfalls of Having Sex Before Love

Having sex before love sends a clear message. It communicates to men that you don't have boundaries or standards and that you don't know what you want (or that you are only interested in sex, which may or may not even be the case). Instead of being in control, knowing what you want and understanding the falling in love process, you appear to be putting sex before love, and that thwarts the process. Here are just some of the pitfalls of having sex without love.

1) **Breeds Fear and Insecurity:** Instead of feeling in control, strong, confident, playful, energized, and stable—all of which are required in order for him to fall in love and for you to be able to keep your wits about you—sex before love typically breeds insecurity and fear. How could you possibly feel secure about the relationship if you have no idea how he truly feels about you (or you about him)? Or if you have no idea where the relationship is going? You may have gotten an *impression* from this man during the brief time you've spent together, but you could be seriously mistaken and end up disillusioned. It happens all the time.

Helena, 42, shared her story with me. "I noticed that I feel confident and in charge when a man is initially chasing me. But once I have sex I get scared and I start to act differently. I wonder when (or if) he's going to call, and I feel like bringing up the subject of the relationship so I can get reassurance that he is still into me… it definitely has thrown off my game and made me insecure. And then it never fails—the guy starts to pull away and then I act even more insecure! It's awful. But why do I keep doing it? I don't know!"

I cover the "whys" in another chapter, but ultimately *why* it is happening is not nearly as important as simply making the decision to put the behavior behind you and committing to doing things differently from now on. To build a rock solid relationship you need to be confident, strong, clear, and in control, so make a commitment to yourself to put love before sex next time. Also, I go into this more later, but just know that it is never okay to call a man, other than to return his call. This all changes once you're in a committed, monogamous relationship and you're both in love, but during the courting stage, don't call him.

2) **Prevents You From Getting to Know Each Other**: It takes a long time to truly get to know a person. Think about it—doesn't it seem strange and even outrageous to sleep with a man you may have only known for a few days or weeks? It really is putting the cart before the horse, because once you

Love Before Sex

have sex with the person, either he disappears, or it becomes a sort of "situation" (as opposed to a real relationship, which has clear-cut boundaries and conditions). You do get to know the person as you continue to spend time with him but something is lost.

Keeping sex out of the picture allows for a different kind of relating that forces you to go deeper with each other. Instead of getting side-tracked and caught up in the passion and physical aspect of the relationship, you get creative and start to explore each others' minds, hearts, dreams, goals, fears, and so on. A foundation begins to develop that will serve you for a very long time, even a lifetime, if he's the one. *Hannah, 27,* explains how this worked for her. "With my last two boyfriends I noticed that we got to know each other *after* we had sex. It didn't take long to figure out we weren't compatible on so many levels! But we had already become so intimate that we felt obligated to try to make it work. But we just couldn't because we weren't right for each other. I couldn't believe how little I knew about them."

3) **You Lose His Interest/Respect**: Realize that this is not always the case, but I think we all know enough examples of it happening—whether to you personally, or to someone you know. If you have sex on the first few dates, there's a good chance the guy will lose interest and respect. In contrast, when you put love before sex, you get a man's attention because you stand out as unique and different. You know who you are, what you want, and you won't settle. You take care of yourself and don't allow just anyone, especially someone you barely know, to have too much of you too soon. You value yourself too much. You protect your heart,

Chapter 2 How Sex Before Love Sabotages True Love

soul/spirit, body, and you don't make yourself available to someone who doesn't love you or who hasn't proven himself to you. No one could have the impression that you are *easy*. You aren't frigid or uptight—you simply reserve yourself for someone who deserves you. It isn't that you are trying to be seen as the virtuous "good girl" because you believe that is what men want (although that is what men want, when it comes to *marrying* a girl). It is more about the fact that you are too smart to give so much of yourself to someone so early in the dating process. You aren't playing games; you're simply taking care of yourself. *Rachel*, 39, shared her experience. "I hate the whole double-standard, but hey, it's reality. As much as I hoped that the guy would still be crazy about me after having sex for the first time, it just never works that way. It's like they think less of you after that."

We could focus on the notion that men are jerks in this area and that it isn't fair. But I think it's wiser to instead focus on the solution. Let's first strive to understand how men think and how they are different from women, and then understand how men fall in love and what conditions are necessary for love to grow. The key point to remember above all is: he must be in love before you have sex. Love *before* sex—no matter what. How to facilitate that love comes later in the book.

4) <u>You Lose Control</u>: As a woman, your sexuality is your power. When you have sex too soon you give up your power, on many levels. The chase is over. Keeping sex at bay helps to maintain the heightened level of intensity that makes a new relationship so exciting. Once you have sex, it's over and you are left with something much less valuable than what you really want (however, if you are both in love, then having sex *enhances* the relationship). It can go in a variety of directions, but none are quite what you dreamt of when you thought about spending your life with the man you love. It could be nothing but a one-night-stand, or a *two*-night-stand, or a *few-weeks*-stand, or a *few-months*-stand—all of which equal mediocrity and lacking true, solid, real love that can last a lifetime. You may have gotten caught up with the wrong guy for *years* as a result of having sex too soon, which led to you being in a "situation" that you tried hard to make work. But you want a relationship that can last a lifetime and that is based on true love, and you don't want to waste any more time with the wrong men.

Candace, 59, can relate. "I knew immediately that I lost my power if I had sex early on with a guy. If you're waiting by the phone and canceling plans with your girlfriends at the last minute to be with him, and doing other crazy and desperate things just to be with him when he decides to make time for you, then you know you've lost your power." The powerful truth is that you don't have to lose your power. You don't have to have sex with the men you date. You get to keep your power, and you do it by saying no to sex. Forever? No—of course not! But it's a solid "No" until he is in love and willing to make a commitment to be exclusive.

5) **The pacing of the relationship is thrown off**: As the woman, *you* pace the relationship and you do it through keeping sex out of the picture until everything is in place. You probably already know based on experience that he is not going to take on this crucial role in the dating process. Most men are going to go as far as you let them go. There are exceptions, and I'm finding this more and more these days (with women becoming more sexually aggressive than ever before). And I'm not demonizing men—I'm simply

acknowledging what women have been experiencing all their lives! However, more and more *men* are also admitting that sex can complicate matters and they too would like to build a strong foundation and get to know the woman better. Despite this, most men are still not going to be the ones to put the brakes on during the hot and heavy make-out sessions. That's your job. Embrace it and be grateful that you possess the power to pace the relationship and direct it the way you want.

Stacey, 36, saw how this happened in her current relationship. "My boyfriend acts like it's too soon to move forward in our relationship, even though we've been together for nine months. I mean, we have been sleeping together almost that entire time. It seems like the relationship should move forward, from one stage to the next. But we just stay stuck. It's so frustrating." Sound familiar? Stacey is right—there are stages of a relationship and part of every woman's job is to guide the relationship through those stages (artfully letting the guy think *he* is the one coming up with the idea of moving forward!), paying special attention to the pacing and timing of moving through each stage. Sex too soon (before love) takes away your ability to pace the relationship. You don't want to get side-tracked into what I call "no-man's land", wherein there are only situations, not healthy relationships.

6) ***The Foundation isn't Solid; therefore the Relationship Doesn't Develop Properly:*** Consider the foundation of a home. You know the importance of having a solid foundation in order to support the home for as long as it's standing. The better the foundation, the longer it stands, and the better and more secure you'll feel as the homeowner. Same thing with a relationship. You want a foundation that is so solid that it can withstand any stormy weather, ups and downs, major life challenges, and so on. What is the foundation made up of? Here are just a few things, in no particular order:

a. Deep feelings of love

b. A lifetime commitment to be exclusive

c. The willingness to make it legal

d. A clear understanding of give and take and what each person is willing to contribute

e. A history of time together spent going through a variety of life experiences

f. Trust, honesty, compassion for each other a sincere concern for each others' welfare

g. Chemistry/Passion

Is it even possible to create this kind of a foundation if you have sex with the person within days or weeks of meeting him? A case could be made that you can have sex whenever you want and then continue to build the foundation over time. But, as we have been discussing, sex often derails the process, thwarts feelings, clouds the issues, and complicates the entire journey. A much stronger foundation can be built if sex is postponed during the foundation-building period. Think of that time as your window for building your rock solid foundation that is going to support your relationship of a lifetime.

Pamela, 57, did this and it paid off. "I have definitely made tons of mistakes when I was younger, but when I met Keith I knew I wanted to play my cards right. He was so charming and such a nice guy. I knew he'd make a great dad. So I wouldn't jump into bed right away. I said I wanted more than just a sex partner. And I asked him if that's all he was looking for. I made it very clear that if that's what he wanted, he was with the wrong lady. That seemed to make him sit up to attention and he immediately said that he wanted more too. We fell in love and got married within a year."

It doesn't always work this way, of course, but quite often it does. The chances of the relationship transitioning smoothly from stage to stage, leading to love and marriage, goes up exponentially, in my opinion, if you follow these guidelines. It may take awhile to meet the one you want, but once you do and it's a good match, your chances for success are great.

7) **You can Get Hurt:** I am not saying that all women who have casual sex will feel badly about it. And I'm not saying that they *should* feel shame as a result of having casual sex. As I have said before, this is not a moral message—I have no problem with anyone consciously choosing to have sex whenever they want to have sex (it all depends on what you really want and what your own personal values are!). But the reality is that there are many women who *do* feel shame as it relates to their sexual history and experiences, for a variety of reasons. I get letters from women all over the world who have felt used, taken advantage of, misled by men who they thought cared about them. For many women, giving of themselves sexually is a big deal and it hurts them deeply when they share so much of themselves, only to have the relationship not last.

Love Before Sex

A religious upbringing strongly influences some women, even if they don't continue to espouse those beliefs. If you were raised to believe that you are committing a serious sin by having sex outside of marriage (fornication) —it can take a long time to unwind those tapes and instill new beliefs. Also, something like 1 in 4 girls will be sexually abused at some point in their life—there is no doubt that these sexual experiences can trigger intense feelings that connect with those earlier experiences. All the more reason to protect your emotions and make sure you put love before sex and take your time getting to know the person with whom you allow yourself to be so vulnerable.

Lucy, 53, was abused as a child and has struggled with this all her life. "As a teenager, I was very promiscuous because of the childhood abuse. I just thought that's what I had to do to get the guy's love. Then I learned better, but my self-esteem still wasn't up to par so I continued to give in sooner than I really wanted to. Let's just say I went against my intuition because I really didn't know how to say no. You would think that being in my 50s would give me the wisdom and ability to do it right—but I'm still affected by the abuse and don't know how to make a relationship work."

Even if you don't have any former trauma or painful experiences affecting you, casual sex tends to be unfulfilling in general. You may disagree and there certainly are plenty of women out there who enjoy a good romp in the sack and seem to be able to separate themselves emotionally from the experience. But the point of this book is to help you break the cycle of dead-end relationships by putting sex off until you know, love, and trust the person.

Libby, 27, has been dating Mark, 35, for one year. They hit it off immediately and both marveled at how well

Chapter 2 How Sex Before Love Sabotages True Love

they got along. This fast bonding led Libby to believe that Mark's feelings were more developed than they really were, which made her feel comfortable enough to have sex on the 4th date ("It seemed like so much longer than that!" she said). He said things like, "I've never felt this way about someone before", and often made references to the future, as though he was planning on them being together for a long time. She was thinking marriage, despite it only being the 4th date, but Mark, of course, never brought up the subject. When she brought it up he would say things like, "It's too soon for that." Libby decided to give it another 6 months, after which she brought up the subject again. "I felt like I was begging him to love me—to prove that he loved me enough to fully commit to me," she said. His response never changed. He wasn't ready to get married and he finally admitted that he didn't love her "that way."

When asked to retrace her steps and look at when they became sexual, Libby realized that she didn't discuss anything before having sex (such as commitment, feelings for each other, future goals, etc.) because "... it seemed so obvious that we were falling in love and that we were going to be in a relationship." This particular situation highlights a common mistake that women make: they allow themselves to get caught up in the excitement/romance of it all and they buy into the fantasy. For example, when a woman hears references to the future, or the guy makes comments that lead them to believe that the man is "falling" for them, they often take this far more seriously than they should. It isn't necessarily that the men are lying (although some do), but they too get caught up in the romance and passion and they say things that they may very well feel in that moment. But that doesn't mean it's real and lasting.

Love Before Sex

The business of love is a serious one and you have to keep your head together. If it's only been 3 dates, it doesn't matter what is said or how fabulous a time you are having—you don't know this person and you need to rein it in and stay in control. Enjoy yourself but don't take it all so seriously. Definitely don't get a false sense of security and sleep with him—remember, you just met this person and it takes a very long time to get to know the real him, and vice versa. Enjoy the flirty banter if it comes up over time, but realize that it's just part of the process in a new relationship—it doesn't necessarily mean anything at this point. You still have to have the Pre-sex Pow-Wow (Chapter 3) and cover all of the important topics—*before* having sex.

Hopefully it is becoming clearer and clearer that sex before love sabotages real love. You have to ask yourself, if it's *love* you want, then why settle for just sex? And the follow up question to that would be, when *is* it okay to say yes to sex? Read on to find out...

Chapter 3
The Big Pow-Wow: What to Say and How to Say it

The time <u>has finally</u> arrived to establish your sexual boundaries, and in the process, create the space for true love to develop. This is the most exciting time in the dating process because it's when you separate the men from the boys, so to speak. A shift is created in the energy and direction of the relationship, *based on you saying no to his sexual advances*, which allows the *possibility* of falling in love to begin. It is still only a possibility, but it is at this point that the men who are not keepers are weeded out. As we've discussed, there is always a chance that the guy you are seeing is only interested in getting down your pants, and so those particular men will hit the road. And good riddance! At least you won't be having sex with them and feeling like a fool afterward. You are too smart for that now, and you are playing for keeps. You have put the one-night-stands (or two-nights, three-nights, etc.) behind you, and you're finished with the serial monogamy game. By the time you finish reading this book you are going to be "armed and dangerous" with all of the tools necessary to capture his heart and negotiate a commitment.

In this chapter you will learn why it's crucial to have the Pow-Wow (before becoming sexual with the guy), when the appropriate time is to have the Pow-Wow, what your own Pre-

Sex Pow-Wow spiel will be, and how to deliver it. There will also be some variations of the typical Pre-Sex Pow-Wow conversation that you can consider. Sound frightening? *Maria,* 24, thought so. "When I first heard about the idea of a Pow-Wow I thought it was nuts…how in the world can I say those things, that soon in the relationship?! But then as I thought about it, I realized, Why not? Why wouldn't I have the right to speak up for myself and be able to say no to sex if it seems like it's too soon? It dawned on me that I was just afraid. Afraid of what he would say or do or think of me. And that's pretty lame, if you think about it."

Why the Pow-Wow is so Important

This is the most important discussion you will have with the man you are seeing because it will set the foundation for your entire relationship. Think about it: this is when you are laying the ground rules for how he is to proceed if he wants to continue seeing *you.* This is a defining moment in the relationship, in which you are teaching him how you want to be treated, what type of relationship you are available for, and the type of relationship for which you are *not* available. You are not playing games or trying to manipulate him—in fact, you are being your most honest self. You are telling him exactly what you want (in *general* that is—you don't want it to seem like you have already decided you want *him*) and what you are willing to give at this point in the relationship (which is nothing sexually, at this point).

Chapter 3 The Big Pow Wow: What to Say and How to Say It

Here is the breakdown of why having the Pow-Wow is so important:

1. **Protects You:** no smooth-talker with objectionable intentions can seduce you and lead you down a dead-end path. It just won't happen because you're too smart for that—you take things too slowly, and you have certain standards that a man must live up to in order to have you. Only someone truly interested and with the best of intentions will stick around and accept your standards. So, this approach protects you from getting majorly hurt. No one likes to feel used or duped. And while plenty of other women are blaming the men for their misfortune—you are taking full responsibility for your life and exercising proper precautions to ensure that the man you are seeing really has potential.

2. **Establishes Boundaries:** as mentioned earlier, having the Pow-Wow sets your standard for the relationship. It is a crucial part of the foundation-building process—in fact; it's one of the most defining moments of the entire relationship. *It is your most obvious moment to deliberately lay out your true values and heart's desires.* The man is asking for a good time in the sheets and you are saying, "Whoa—not so fast! Hold on to your knickers there buddy and let's have a little chat." You are then letting him know that you are not someone to take lightly. You don't just give yourself away without any thought or discussion or requirements. You are communicating that you care about yourself enough to stand up for yourself and make sure that your needs are met. And you don't just have *sexual* needs in the moment—you have *emotional* needs as well. He needs to know that to have you he must be game for a full-on commitment to be exclusive, with marriage as

59

the goal (or wherever you ultimately want the relationship to go), and he has to love you. It is a lot, but you're worth it. If he isn't sure enough about that, then he has a couple of choices: continue non-sexually, until he is sure—or move on. Simple as that.

3. **Creates Space for True Love to Grow**: Have you ever given much thought to how it is that a man falls in love with a woman? It is a mystery that humans have tried to solve since the beginning of time. I delve further into this subject in chapter 10, but the main point here is that when you refuse to give of yourself sexually, you create a challenge that not only piques a man's interest, but that also begins the falling-in-love process. *It is that intense longing for you but not being able to have you that ignites the whole process.* But it isn't only because he wants you sexually and can't have you—it is also because he begins to develop a deeper respect for you and your values. He sees that you are a woman of character and someone who values herself. This is the kind of woman he could love, marry, and with whom he could have children. He could count on a woman like this—she would be loyal, faithful, and honorable. She isn't the type who would compromise herself for some brief pleasure or fun. So, it is the combination of desperately and passionately wanting this woman who is withholding—*and* developing respect for her as she stands true to herself. Men find this fascinating. On one hand they become *enamored* with a woman who is elusive, and yet they *revere* her for being unyielding as it relates to her moral integrity.

4. **Creates Structure for the Relationship**: if you don't have the Pow-Wow before you bring sex into the picture,

Chapter 3 The Big Pow Wow: What to Say and How to Say It

your relationship lacks structure. Are you exclusive? Are you working towards any goals? How do you feel about each other and have those feelings been clearly expressed? What are your expectations for each other, and for the relationship? Are you going to see each other every weekend, or occasionally, or move in together? If you don't have the Pow-Wow and clarify these and other points you risk stepping into a "situation". You sleep with him and then you go home and wonder when he's going to call again, or when you will see him again. You wonder if he's falling in love or if that was it. Insecurity sets in, confusion and unmatched expectations create tension and unhappiness. All of this is unnecessary if you have the Pow-Wow and create clear parameters for the relationship. It may not be the sexiest conversation you'll ever have, but it will give you piece of mind and allow you to put your focus on enjoying the relationship versus having to manage your anxiety.

5. **Prevents You From Bonding Emotionally:** When you are establishing the foundation for your relationship you need to have a clear head. If your emotions are clouded as a result of Oxytocin you limit your ability to make wise choices and you're less likely to dot all of the I's and cross all of the T's. This is why it's called the *Pre-Sex* Pow-Wow—you discuss the important points *before* you get swept away and enveloped in an Oxytocin bath. You can enjoy sex all the more when you have the cerebral part of the process out of the way.

When to Have the Pow-Wow

The Pow-Wow only needs to happen when he makes a sexual advance. Why? Because that is when he is *asking something of you*. He is asking quite a lot, actually. He's asking you to get naked with him and to allow him to enter your body and share the most intimate experience two people can have together. It is only because he is asking for something so private, special, intimate, powerful, and emotionally bonding, that you have the right/responsibility to respond in a thoughtful and self-protecting way.

If you bring up the points in the Pow-Wow before he makes a sexual advance you risk looking foolish, and as if you are trying too hard to move the relationship forward. This can make you seem desperate, which then confuses the guy and makes him wonder if you're a great catch. You never want to be the one to bring up highly-charged topics such as the future of the relationship, your relationship goals/dreams, feelings for each other, and the like. *He* must be the one to bring up these subjects, because he is the pursuer.

If you say yes to his sexual advances without having the Pow-Wow, you miss the perfect opportunity to discuss these crucial points and it then becomes awkward to attempt to bring up the points at a later date. If you do, you can unfairly be seen as a nag or pressuring him to marry you, which feels demeaning. However, if you are simply responding to his advances, then you are perfectly within your right to have this discussion, and you come off as a wise, thoughtful woman who has her act together. You didn't initiate the conversation—*he* initiated it by asking you to get naked with him. Otherwise you would have been fine just enjoying the date!

What to Say and How to Say it

You may have had brief, casual conversations up to this point in which you may have given this guy some indication that you don't jump into sex quickly...but men these days are used to women saying things like this

Chapter 3 The Big Pow Wow: What to Say and How to Say It

without really meaning it. Men know that "no" doesn't necessarily mean "*no*"—it often just means that they have to try a little harder. Some women like to give the impression they're "good girls" and prefer to make it seem like they only gave in because the man was too hard to resist. But you don't play games like this and you mean what you say. This is too serious to take lightly and you are not a frivolous person when it comes to this subject—at least not at this point in your life.

So, the typical scenario is that you are kissing passionately and then his hand ends up on your breast. Whatever the situation, it is obvious that he is attempting to take this little make-out session to the next level. That's your cue. You gently remove his hand from your breast, or gently push him away, and say something like this (make sure that everything you say is honest—don't ever say something that you don't really feel/think):

"_____, we need to talk about a few things. I want you to know that I am very attracted to you, and I really do like you. And I'm also a sexual person. But I take sex very seriously. I know this may sound old-fashioned, but I believe that it's best to be in love before I make love. <u>Sex complicates everything and makes it harder to really get to know the person—and we are just barely getting to know each other.</u> I also want something that is real and lasting and based on all the right things—like love, commitment, trust, respect, and a real understanding of each other. And I believe that sex needs to be put on the back burner for awhile in order for that to develop, if it is going to develop at all. <u>I hope you can respect how I feel. I know it's difficult because of the chemistry between us,</u> but if we both want to take this relationship seriously and see where it goes, then I know we can do it."

I strongly suggest you memorize this little spiel (after you tweak it so that it sounds like you). Pretend that it's an important speech you have to give in front of millions of people—practice it at least ten times so you don't flub up when you're in the moment. You don't want to seem nervous or like you are unsure of what you're saying. You want it to flow off your tongue and come from your heart in the most sincere way possible.

Variations of the Pow-Wow

There are a couple of variations of this conversation that you can use. For example, you may want to give less information initially and wait for him to elicit that information. So, instead of saying the part about wanting to be "in love before making love", you could leave that out and wait for him to ask the question: "When *will* you be willing to have sex?" The point is that you are making it clear that *now* is not the right time—it is way too soon. He must respect that and you don't owe him any further explanation, really. But at some point during the courtship all of the points outlined in this chapter need to be made. It's up to you in terms of when you say it all. In general it's good to be a bit mysterious and reveal the details of your position slowly, over time. But you don't want to seem like a tease, or as if you are playing games. Once a man understands your true reasons for wanting to postpone sex, he will respect you for them.

WHAT IS YOUR STANDARD?

One definition of standard is "A level of quality or attainment". For example, "The restaurant requires a high standard of service." We all have standards, whether we are

Chapter 3 The Big Pow Wow: What to Say and How to Say It

conscious of them or not. When you determine what you standard will be, you are establishing your criteria—it is what is required of someone who wants to become intimate with you. This is something that needs to be determined by you, for you, without anyone else interfering. This is a very personal matter that is extremely serious. You are deciding when it's okay for you to be as intimate as you can be with another human being, as well as other important criteria, which we will cover here.

Your standard is also something that remains steady and consistent. It's your "standard of living" so to speak, and so you don't flip flop or change your mind, depending on how hot he is or how special the relationship seemed to be when you just met. It's your values, morals, and way of being. People who come into your life either accept them, or they don't. But once you determine what's truly right for you, your standard never wavers.

Men are capable of "setting the sexual standard" in a relationship, but it is usually the woman who decides when sex is going to happen. I do hear more and more, however, that men are putting the brakes on sex too soon, because women are just so sexually aggressive these days. It works in your favor ladies, for the *man* to make the sexual moves and you put on the brakes. It gives you that opportunity to discuss the relationship and where it's going. It puts you in the driver's seat and it creates the momentum you need to move the relationship forward. So sit back and let him make the moves, and be patient if it takes a long time. Eventually he will make a move. Don't try to rush it.

There are three different Standards from which to choose: <u>Commitment, Engagement, or Marriage</u>. Spend some time pondering each of these standards and consider your religious beliefs, feelings, and goals. Don't worry about society or how men or others might react. This is just for you.

Standard #1: Requiring a Commitment

With a commitment, both persons verbally agree not to date other people. You also verbally agree on the direction of the relationship. Most people want to get married, but not necessarily. Perhaps you want a committed, monogamous relationship that lasts a lifetime but you're not interested in getting legally married. It's up to you to tailor the relationship to what you want it to be. Just be careful... I've known a few women who thought they didn't want marriage, only to realize that they really did prefer the full commitment of marriage, only to be upset that the men wouldn't change their positions. In any case, the goals and direction of the relationship must be very clear. Many misunderstandings have occurred simply because the exact terms of the commitment were not spelled out clearly enough. Both persons should understand that the relationship may not end up in marriage (you are willing to take that risk), but if marriage is the goal, that must be crystal clear.

I would also suggest that you establish a date—say 9-12 months out—whereby you discuss moving the relationship forward to getting engaged, or you discuss other alternatives, such as going your separate ways or postponing the date in order to give you more time to think about it.

Chapter 3 The Big Pow Wow: What to Say and How to Say It

Sample Conversation

YOU: *It's important to me that I be in a committed, monogamous relationship with the person I'm sexual with...I want to know that my partner loves me, and vice versa. It doesn't make sense to me to jump into sex and then get to know someone. So I hope you can be patient and are willing to put sex off for awhile, while we get to know each other and see how our feelings develop.*

HIM: *Wow, that's pretty stringent. I have no idea how I feel at this point...do you have a time frame in mind?*

YOU: *I know it's a different way to approach relationships. And I don't have an exact time frame in mind. It's more about how we feel about each other and what we both want. I eventually want to be in a committed, monogamous relationship that leads to marriage. I'm not in a rush to make that happen, but I'm not comfortable bringing sex into the picture until I at least know that we are on the same page in terms of our feelings and the direction of the relationship. I take sex very seriously because I tend to bond emotionally and I don't want to do that with just anyone, especially if I have no idea how he feels about me.*

Standard #2: Requiring Formal Engagement

Under this Standard, you don't have sex until you're formally engaged—with a ring and a wedding date set. The advantage of this Standard is that you have even more confirmation that he loves you and that he is committed to the goal of marriage. Remember to set that date!

Sample Conversation

YOU: *I happen to take sex very seriously, and although I do not feel the need to wait until I am married, I do plan to wait until I'm engaged. I just don't want to be sexually involved with someone again until I know I am going to spend the rest of my life with that person.*

HIM: *I am not into casual sex either, but to wait until we are engaged could take a long time!*

YOU: *I agree, but it shouldn't take us an enormous length of time, if that's what we both want in general. Most people know fairly early in the relationship whether or not they could marry that person. I just don't want sex to get in the way of us being able to discover our true feelings. I don't want to rush into getting married, but I also don't want to rush into having sex. We can put off having sex for awhile—it's not going to kill us.*

Standard #3: Requiring Marriage

Under this standard, you do not have sex until you are legally married. Believe it or not, there are still plenty of people out there who want until marriage to become sexual. It may be rare, and typically it is due to religious beliefs, but it is the choice for some. The advantage here is that you are guaranteed full commitment prior to sharing so much of yourself—therefore you are more secure and you know your partner really loves you for you.

Sample Conversation

YOU: *I feel that sex is a very sacred, special act that should be shared between two people who are married. Although I'm not a virgin, my values have changed. It's very*

Chapter 3 The Big Pow Wow: What to Say and How to Say It

important for me to be with a man who can accept my feelings about this. (You can also share your religious beliefs, or whatever other reasons you might have for choosing this Standard).

HIM: *I do feel very strongly about you, but I can't say that I am ready to propose marriage. That takes a long time to determine, and I'm not sure how we can have a relationship for that long without having sex as a part of it. Besides, since you're not a virgin, I feel like somewhat of a fool to wait when you haven't in the past.*

YOU: *I know this may be new for you, but it means a lot to me. I realize that we are a long way from considering marriage. But I'm in no hurry and I know we can postpone sex for awhile and just focus on getting to know each other. If you're serious about me then you'll be able to do it. And if you don't want to, then I guess we're not a good match. And although these were not always my values, they are my values today. I hope that you can accept this about me, but if not, I understand.*

IMPORTANT ISSUES TO CONSIDER PRIOR TO BEING PHYSICAL

Regardless of which Standard you choose, important issues must be discussed before being physical. We will cover more about how to get a commitment in chapter 8, but you will need to make sure all of these points are carefully considered before getting physical.

- **How You Feel About Him.** Since women usually determine their feelings quicker than men in relationships, most women will already know if there is potential by the time he makes advances. Yet, many women become so obsessed with getting *him* to commit that they forget about considering if they even want to be exclusive themselves! Ask yourself these questions: 1) am I in love with him (or at least falling in love)? Have we talked about compatibility issues (see chapter 9), would I want to marry this man (and have his children, etc.)?

- ***How He Feels About You.*** Ideally a man will express his true feelings for you before he makes any sort of sexual advance. But unfortunately, it usually doesn't work out that way. Typically the man makes the moves and you aren't really sure how he feels, or he may have given you the impression that he's really into you, but he may not have expressed genuine feelings. He needs to know that you would never become sexual with anyone who didn't love you. *Do not ask him directly if he loves you. And never, ever say "I love you" before he does.* You are simply letting him know your standard. You aren't requiring anything of him at this point, so if he jumps to that conclusion be sure and set him straight.

    You can say, "I'm not expecting you to tell me you love me or anything. I'm just saying that it's important for me to be *in love* before I *make love,* and I want my partner to feel the same. I'm in no rush, and maybe that won't happen for us, but that's just how I feel." He can then think about it and he will know that if he doesn't already love you, he will have to just continue dating you until those feelings develop or he'll move on. But the key point here is that he has to be in love with you and he has to express those feelings prior to becoming sexual.

- ***The Amount of Time You Spend Together.*** You will want to consider how much time together you need to be comfortable. Some men will say they want a serious relationship but as you go along you realize they only want to see you on the weekends or every other week. This is another reason why you want to take it slow—so that you can see his rhythms and how often he wants to see you. Before you become sexual you will want to be clear about the amount of time you will spend together. You don't need to come out and directly ask how much time he plans to spend with you (he probably won't know the answer to that anyway), but just watch and see how often he calls and how often he wants to get together and see if you are comfortable with it. If you feel lonely in the relationship and are always wondering when or if he's going to call, the last thing you will want to do is sleep with him because that shortage of time together will only get worse, most likely. A common scenario is that you spend a lot of time together in the beginning of the relationship, but shortly thereafter the time together becomes less and less. It's up to you to take care of yourself and determine what your needs are and whether or not he can meet them.

- ***The Future.*** This is a very important point to consider because no matter how strongly you feel about him or how much time you spend together, if you are thinking marriage and he is not, you've got a problem. You are stuck in a relationship that becomes stagnant. You are both at a stalemate and you are usually the one who gets the worse deal. So before being sexual, you should discuss the future and his intentions. More than anything watch his actions. You can intuitively know if a man is really serious about you. The way he treats you makes it obvious. If you choose Standard #1 (Commitment), and you have made your commitment to be exclusive, then establish a time—say, several months to a year—when you both will sit down and discuss moving on to the next level (engagement). If you are choosing Standard #2 simply choose a wedding date. If you both agree on a time limit, then you avoid having the relationship drag on forever.

- ***Length of Time You Have Been Together.*** Before becoming sexual with him you will also want to consider how long you've been seeing this person. The truth is, you could date someone for six months and have a lesser degree of love and commitment than a couple who has been together for only six weeks. Although it rarely happens, there are couples who meet and fall deeply in love almost immediately. You can cover a lot of ground in a short period of time and determine that you want the same things in life and that you are ready for a serious relationship. I do believe, however, that to fully get to know someone takes time. So although the feelings may seem strong early on and everything seems like a go, the longer you take to fully get to know each other, the better. I suggest at least one year.

HOW TO TELL IF HE IS BEING HONEST

Unfortunately, there are men who will say whatever it takes to have sex with you. It's hard to believe anyone would do this, but it happens all the time. Some men clearly are

Chapter 3 The Big Pow Wow: What to Say and How to Say It

just out for one thing. Others may make a commitment to be exclusive with every intention of keeping that commitment only to discover that their feelings have changed. It happens, and it's a risk you take when you have sex early on in the dating process. Here are a few warning signs that he's only in it for the sex:

- He only wants to come over or wants you to come over to his place.
- He is very touchy right away (puts his hand on your waist, touches your hair a lot, etc.).
- He makes very aggressive physical advances right away (within the first couple of dates).
- He acts like he just has to have you and that he will go crazy if he can't have you sexually.
- He asks very personal questions relating to sex, very early in the relationship.
- He tries to change your views about sex, attempting to convince you that you're wrong.
- He is constantly staring at your breasts or other personal areas.
- He does not seem interested in getting to know *you*.
- He strongly encourages you to drink too much or take drugs.

If you suspect that he is only interested in sex, then telling him that you are not available is the wisest thing to do. He may change his ways down the road, but I wouldn't stick around to find out. I think it's better to find a man whose priorities are different. *Taking your time* and being *very observant* can help prevent you from going too far with a man who's only interested in one thing.

Fear of Scaring Him Away

It is at this point that many women cringe, as they imagine themselves having this discussion, and they say things like, "But he's going to think I'm crazy! It's too soon to talk about being in love!" But think about it. Isn't it these *men* who are the crazy ones? To have the nerve to expect sex so soon after meeting you!? Unfortunately, it is the *women* who have spoiled men by giving them sex without love, commitment, or any requirements at all, who are crazy. I want you to really think about this—sit back and ponder the reality of this situation… you have just met this person and have gone out once, twice, three times—maybe even a couple of weeks. You barely know this person and yet he is asking to have access to the most private, personal, intimate part of you. And typically, as a result of having this experience, you bond emotionally with the person and tend to lose a certain amount of control over your feelings, which then affects the way you behave in the relationship, which often ends up sabotaging the entire process and the relationship ends after a few months or even years. And you are willing to do it!

I'm hoping that by thinking deeply about the reality of this you will come to your senses and realize that sex with someone you barely know is not good for you on any level. I don't care how hot the sex is, and how much pleasure you glean from it—you deserve more and can do better. Don't give away all of your power to someone who doesn't even know you (nor do you know him), let alone love you!

If you start to feel nervous and afraid that it's too soon to talk about love, commitment, and goals for the relationship, just remember that the only reason you are bringing up these topics is because he is asking you to have sex with him. All you are doing is giving him an answer and honestly explaining why. He can do what he wants with the information—the ball is in his court at that point. You are not asking anything of him—you are simply being open and honest about how you feel and what you are willing to give at this point, based on the fact that he was asking something of you. And your reasons for saying no are based on your personal values related to taking care of yourself, protecting yourself emotionally, physically, mentally, and so on, from getting too emotionally attached too soon to someone who hasn't yet proved himself to be trustworthy, sincere, and a good match.

You are essentially telling him that you don't take sex lightly, that you move slowly when it comes to sex, that you take good care of yourself and that you're not easy. Why should you be the least bit nervous about conveying this message to him? It's your body and your life—you have every right! Actually, you have an *obligation*, to yourself. No one else is going to protect you, stand up for you, and ensure that *your* needs are met. That's up to you. Trust me, very few men, if any, are going to stop mid-make-out-session and say, "Um, you know, we are moving way too fast here and I don't want you to get hurt because at this point I'm not really sure how I feel about you. In fact, I may not ever call you again. So, let's stop this now and focus on getting to know each other better first. We can always have sex after we fall in love." It may have happened to someone out there, but not to anyone I've ever known. So embrace your role as self-caregiver and do the best job you can for yourself.

Love Before Sex

Let me make a bold promise to you: the chances that you will lose men because you require love before sex is extremely slim. You may lose men for all kinds of other reasons—he doesn't want to be exclusive, he's not attracted to you, he's in love with someone else, he doesn't like the way you chew your food or he hates your cats... there are so many potential reasons why he will hit the road and not continue to pursue you. But it won't be because you want to put sex on the back burner until you get to know each other better and build a real relationship—unless of course, that was all he was interested in the first place. In which case, you should be elated that you didn't sleep with him. If you don't have any experience in this area, then you just have to trust my years of experience—men, in general, are not only fine with waiting to have sex, they actually find it refreshing and intriguing. They may also find it frustrating, maddening, annoying, and difficult—but if they think you're worth it, they will respectfully agree to wait and move forward with the dating process. So, the last thing you need to be worried about is losing men because of having the Pow-Wow. Having the Pow-Wow will only work in your favor. It will only enhance the relationship, and it will enhance you. So hold your head up high and have the Pow-Wow with confidence!

Chapter 4
Responding to His Advances without Bruising His Ego

When it comes to sex, men can be very persuasive. "Come on, let's just lie down for awhile and watch TV. We don't have to do anything!" They may be denied gracefully a few times in the beginning of a relationship but at some point, they will resort to every line, gimmick, plea, or protest known to women. You will need some strong comebacks and solid arguments in place to be prepared. Remember the decision you made to stop the cycle of getting involved with the wrong men and wasting your precious time. It was a good, sound decision and you must stick to it to the end! Remember your goal—to find the right guy and to have him be deeply, crazy in love with you. *Not having sex until he is in love is the key to the entire process*, so don't give in no matter what! This isn't easy, by any means. You will struggle and so will he. There will be times when you will think, "Ok, this is getting ridiculous. We've been seeing each other for a while now and it's obvious that he's crazy about me..." But don't give in to these ideas! *At least several months need to pass; he has to be in love and verbally express his feelings; and all of the Pow-Wow points need to be addressed and locked down.* Don't lose sight of the fact that this is a major factor in *how he falls in love*.

Love Before Sex

In this chapter you will find all of the various lines that men use to get women into bed, as well as specific comebacks with which to respond, along with some main points to remember. I'm sure there are plenty of lines I'm unfamiliar with so please feel free to send me any lines you have heard that aren't in the book!

The Lines Men Use

No doubt you have heard a plethora of lines from men who were trying to get you to fool around. Now that you are putting love before sex, you will be hearing even more of them. You need to be prepared and have your own comebacks in place so that you can keep a cool head in hot situations. Here are just some of the most common lines men use, along with potential responses from you. The responses differ based on whether you want to wait until you are committed, engaged, or married to have sex:

Line: "Sex is a natural part of a relationship"

Response: "I agree. But for *me*, it's a natural part of a *committed* relationship. I want to be *in* love before I *make* love, and I want my partner to feel the same way. I don't want us to us to rush into a commitment, but I'm also unwilling to rush into sex."

Line: "I'm a very sexual guy, there's no way I can't be physical."

Response: "I understand how difficult it must be for you, and it is for me too. But I can't go against my feelings. I'd rather miss out on the temporary satisfaction I'd get by having sex now than miss out on the possibility of building a solid, lasting relationship." (You need to be confident

Chapter 4 Responding to His Advances without Bruising His Ego

enough to say, "Maybe I'm not the right woman for you" if he persists).

Line: "But it's too soon to talk about marriage, love, and all of that!"

Response: "The only reason those subjects came up is because you want us to be sexual. I agree that it's too soon to consider marriage—we are just getting to know each other and our feelings haven't had a chance to develop. And maybe they never will! But it's also too soon to have sex. In my opinion, you have the cart before the horse. Let's forget about sex for the time being and just see where the relationship goes. There's plenty of time for sex if our relationship works out. And if you aren't interested in waiting, then I understand. We can be friends." (You always have to be willing to lose him).

Line: "It seems like you're just playing hard to get, or treating this like a business. It's like you're using sex to get me to commit."

Response: "It may appear that way, but I just want to build a really strong relationship that can last—and I believe that if you have sex too soon it can mess everything up and cloud your true feelings. I don't want to get emotionally bonded to someone who doesn't love me, or if I'm not in a committed relationship. I'm just taking care of myself and making sure I don't get attached to the wrong person."

Line: "We won't do anything... I just want to hold you (or kiss you)."

Response: "I would love to get close to you, but I just don't want to put ourselves in a dangerous situation. I'm not ready to become sexual and kissing leads to more."

Line: "Let's watch a movie at my place. I've had a hard day and don't want to go out."

Response: "I'd rather not be alone at your place. I don't feel comfortable with that right now. We can always get together another time." (By the way, there will come a time when you can go to his place, but why put yourself in a tough situation in which you will be highly tempted and one thing could lead to another? This is just temporary.)

Line: "I feel like I'm back in high school! We're adults here."

Response: "Age or maturity isn't the issue here. I'm just not ready. The *relationship* isn't ready. I don't care what age I'm at—I don't ever want to have sex with someone I am just barely getting to know!"

Line: "But I feel like I've known you forever! I feel so strongly about you and it just feels so right!"

Response: "Maybe it does to you, but I need more time. I want to be in love before I make love. I want to really know the man I'm with and know that we love each other and are committed to each other. You and I are not at that place yet." (You could also come right out and ask him if he thinks he's in love with you...but don't necessarily believe it if the answer is yes, if it's really early on in the relationship.)

Line: "But I love you."

Chapter 4 Responding to His Advances without Bruising His Ego

Response: "If you really love me, then you'll respect my feelings when it comes to this. If your love is real, and if my feelings develop in the same way, and it lasts, then there will be plenty of time for us to express that love physically." (You will need to follow your instincts and be able to discern his sincerity when a man tells you he loves you...be sure to go over all of the Pre-sex Pow-Wow points and even then you might want to wait a little longer before jumping in.)

Line: "So, if I told you I loved you and wanted to be exclusive right now, you'd have sex with me?"

Response: "It doesn't work quite like that, sorry. What I'm trying to say to you is that I want to take it very slowly, spending more time getting to know each other (non-sexually, without sex getting in the way), and seeing how the feelings develop naturally. And then we can have the serious conversation about commitment and so on. But this feels rushed."

Line: "But I am committed to you!"

Response: "What does that mean to you?" (Have a discussion about commitment and what that entails, for both of you...commitment means seeing each other exclusively, but feelings of love need to be part of the equation as well and that takes time).

Line: "I'm just so attracted to you, I can't help myself. You drive me crazy."

Response: "I'm attracted to you too, but we're going to have to exert some self-discipline because it will only destroy our relationship if we have sex too soon. Let's not just react to our physical drives. We have the ability to control our bodies and not let them control us."

Line: "But this is the modern world! Everybody does it!"

Response: "I know that everyone is *not* doing it, but even if they were, it doesn't matter to me what others are doing. If you really care about me, you won't pressure me to do something that I don't want to do." (You need to convey the message that you care about *yourself*, which he should respect.)

Line: "If you're not going to do it, then I'll get it somewhere else!"

Response: "Good luck. And don't let the door hit you on the way out!"

Line: "Why can't we just see what happens, play it by ear and let it progress naturally? This isn't a business, you know."

Response: "I agree, we should let the relationship progress naturally. We can take as long as we need to. I'm in no rush. But for me, sex is only possible once I'm in a committed, monogamous relationship. That's nonnegotiable."

Line: "Even marriage isn't a guarantee."

Response (for someone who wants to wait until marriage): "True, but it is the highest level of commitment two people can make. It's the only commitment honored legally and the only one that would make me feel secure enough to give of myself sexually."

Chapter 4 Responding to His Advances without Bruising His Ego

Line: "There's no way I could marry someone without knowing what she is like sexually."

Response #1: "I can see how you would feel that way. I realize it's scary but if two people truly love each other and communicate their emotions, I believe they can create a beautiful sex life in a marriage. We can also get a good sense of how compatible we will be by our touch, kissing, our chemistry, and so on." (Again, you must be willing to say you may not be the right woman for him rather than try to persuade him to see things your way.)

Another Potential Response: "I agree that sex is an important part of a marriage but if two people love and respect each other, sex isn't going to make or break the relationship. You work at creating a wonderful sex life."

Line: "If you really loved me you would do it."

Response: "Do what? Ruin the specialness of our relationship? Go against my values? I feel that if you really loved *me* you wouldn't pressure me to do something that I don't want to do." (You need to convey the message that you care about yourself, which he should respect—and he most likely will, if not now, then later.)

Line: "Your views are just too old-fashioned and outdated."

Response: "I'm sorry you feel that way. I'm sure there are plenty of women out there who will go along with your way, but I'm just not one of them. I see postponing sex temporarily as a way for two people to build a solid foundation of love, respect, trust, and it creates the space to really get to know each other. Sex can cloud feelings

83

and detract people from getting to know each other on other levels. To me, that is never outdated or old-fashioned!"

Line: "But you've already done it before, so what's the difference?"

Response: "I have a different set of values today, and partly because of my past experiences. I just don't want to continue to rack up the number of men I sleep with—I want to be more selective, take my time, make sure I really know and love the person and vice versa...I believe you can always start over and make new/better choices."

Line: "How do I know you're not frigid and that you are a sexual person?"

Response: "I believe you can easily see that I am a very affectionate, warm person. If I had any hang-ups, or lack of desire, I would tell you. Besides, our chemistry speaks for itself."

Line: "How will we know if we're compatible sexually?"

Response: "There are ways of discovering compatibility: by talking about our sexuality—our level of desire, what feels good to us, and what doesn't feel good. We can tell if we're compatible by our kisses and touch. If we truly love each other and are physically attracted to each other, then chances are we will be compatible. We need to believe that we can work things out no matter what and that we can make our sex life great if we want to."

Another Potential Response: "I don't want to wait until marriage, so if we get to the point where we are in

Chapter 4 Responding to His Advances without Bruising His Ego

love, committed to each other exclusively, and have established goals for the relationship, then we will get to that part of the relationship and we will know just how compatible we are!"

Line: "It's unnatural to suppress your sexual urges."

Response: "No one has ever died from not having sex, and besides, it's only temporary! Although we may strongly *desire* to have sex, we don't necessarily *need* to have sex in order to survive."

Main Points to Remember:
Men Can't Argue with Your Feelings

If you continuously bring the conversation back to the fact that it doesn't *feel* right for you to be sexual so soon, or that you would be compromising your values and that would *feel* badly, good men will honor that. If he really cares about you, he wouldn't want you to feel bad on any level. He wants you to be happy and he wants to make you happy! So rather than continuously having an intellectual discussion in which you hash things out—redirect the conversation to how you want to *feel* good about yourself, him, and the relationship, and therefore you must be true to yourself. Even the best of men will put sexual pressure on a woman—but they also will care about your feelings. They may need a reminder, however. For example, you could say something like, "I realize that you are a very sexual person and that you have needs. I have similar needs, but right now I have to be true to myself and I need you to be respectful of my feelings. I'm just not ready and it wouldn't feel good to me *emotionally* to go forward sexually at this point. I hope you understand."

Being Sensitive Without Being a Pushover

It's important to put yourself in his shoes and to be sensitive to the fact that the man you are seeing is sexually attracted to you, and he is naturally driven to be sexual with you. You want him to know that you appreciate his attraction to you, and you'll want to be honest about your attraction to him. Let him know that this isn't personal or due to a lack of interest in sex on your part. But be firm.

TRISTA, 32, said this to the man she was dating, "I'm so glad that you are so attracted to me! And I'm so attracted to you too… I'm looking forward to the time when it feels right to move forward with being physical. I know it's really difficult for you—it is for me too. But it will be so much better if and when our emotions and commitment level are at the right place in order to support a sexual relationship." Trista made it clear that she is attracted to him, and she showed understanding and compassion. She also made it clear that it is only temporary, should things work out.

Can you see how this puts the guy in the position whereby he must go deeper into his feelings to determine where he really wants to go with the relationship? A guy who is able to jump into sex right away doesn't have to do that—he already has all that he wants, and the entire process gets derailed. He becomes satiated, which leads to stagnation. You want *momentum*. You want things to move along at a steady pace, from meeting to dating to falling in love, getting engaged, and then married (or, if marriage isn't your goal, then a loving, committed relationship).

Chapter 4 Responding to His Advances without Bruising His Ego

Keeping sex at bay by responding to his advances in the right way is a huge part of the process.

You Must Be Willing to Lose Him

This is one of the most important, and most difficult, principles for women to follow. So many women chicken out and give in, because they don't want to lose the guy. But they lose out on so much more! Do you want him to love you, or do you want him to LOVE you? Do you want the leftovers, or do you want the GOURMET BANQUET? Do you want the weeds, or do you want the beautiful BOUQUET of FLOWERS? Your mantra needs to be that *you refuse to settle*!

First of all, you are picky and selective, so you are taking your time in determining if this guy is even right for you, worthy of you, and so on. It isn't just about him wanting you—you know it takes a long time to get to know someone, and you want something real and lasting—so you know you need to go slowly and be watchful/careful. You also know that you want a man of high quality and with a sterling character. You want the whole package—a smart, funny, loving, kind, sexy, assertive, successful man. He has to show you that he is that man, and so the pressure is on him to win you over. You will also be presenting yourself to him, but you carry yourself as if you already know you can have just about any man you set your sights on. I don't mean this in an arrogant way, but it is more of a "queenly" attitude (minus the bad attitude and/or spoiled brat edge) that demands respect and admiration. We go into this more in Chapter 13, but for this part of the conversation with him you want to give the impression that you are okay with letting him go if he isn't able to step up to the plate.

You Must Come From a Strong, Confident Place

Men today are used to women saying no without meaning it, and with a little persuasion they get what they want. Talk is cheap, but actions speak louder than words. When you are "laying down the law" so to speak, you have to do so with confidence and clarity. That's why you need to practice and memorize your spiel several times and study this chapter until you feel that you are prepared to respond to anything he throws at you. You don't want to hit him over the head with this stuff and project a tone of, "You're not gettin a piece of this buddy and so don't you even think about it!" Your delivery can be, and ideally is, feminine and soft—but it should be clear that you really mean it. And remember, there's no need to even bring up the subject unless he is making a sexual advance.

Do Not be Deceived

If you both truly love each other and have made a solid commitment (and have no problem with premarital sex) then you might be ready to become sexual with your partner. A word of caution: feelings can change! It can be devastating to finally open yourself up to someone who claims to be head-over-heels only to find out that he was confused, didn't really mean it, or was just in it for the challenge. You may have met a real player who knows just what to say, or he may have been a very nice guy but how was he to know that his feelings would change? When the guy is tenderly caressing you and telling you how much he adores you and wants you forever, it's easy to give in. In

Chapter 4 Responding to His Advances without Bruising His Ego

this precarious and delicate process of falling in love, you really have to be in tune with your inner voice. Your true inner voice will never fail you, if you know how to tap into it and truly listen. If you notice yourself getting all giddy and silly over a guy, try to rein it in and spend some time with yourself in which you get very quiet, and ponder what your inner voice is really telling you. He may be exciting, sexy, and compelling—but is there a part of you that suspects trouble? Are you a bit apprehensive or fearful for some reason? What are your friends telling you? If they tell you you're moving too fast, or they hint around that something may be "off" about him or the situation, then really listen to them and then go within. It won't hurt you or the relationship if you pull back a bit and regroup. If his feelings are sincere and the relationship is meant to be, then he will still be there. Remember, *you* pace the relationship. And that requires the confidence to know when things are moving too fast, despite all the fabulous things he is telling you and the butterflies in your tummy. Keep a cool head, be cautious and watchful, and let your inner voice and higher Self direct the course.

Drawing the Line

You are now well-equipped with a plethora of responses to a variety of lines men use to get you into bed. Obviously you can tweak them to suit your voice and personality. It is the content and spirit of the responses that matters most. You just want to get the primary message across, which is: *I like you and I am attracted to you—however, I don't jump into sex quickly. I like to take my time and I want to build a solid foundation in a potential relationship and I don't want sex to get in the way of that. I'm not playing games—I'm*

Love Before Sex

just taking care of myself, and making the relationship a priority (not just sex). I do enjoy sex, but I'm only interested in having it with the man I love and who loves me.

Love (and marriage, if that's what you want) will be a part of your future, and it will be with a man who respects your feelings and honors your wishes. Don't ever settle for someone who discounts your feelings and constantly tries to talk you out of your most important values. All men are going to be driven by that all-powerful testosterone and make moves on you—you actually want that—but you want to end up with a man who is willing to stick around and who actually respects your position on this subject.

Remember one of the most important points in this book: you must be willing to lose a few men, and you must give the impression that you are willing to lose any or all of them, if they can't respect and accept your standards. Your mantra at this point needs to be: *Good things come to those who wait.* Your next question may be, for how long do I have to wait, and is there *anything* I can do in the meantime? This will be the subject of the next chapter.

Chapter 5
How Far Can You Go?

This question reminds me of a bumper sticker I once saw that said, "How Much Can I Get Away With and Still Get to Heaven?" The answer is, *not much*. "Not even *kissing*?" you might ask. You can engage in some light forms of affection, such as kissing, holding hands, hugging, and even snuggling up to each other under certain circumstances, such as in a movie theatre. But if you are struggling with understanding *why* you must refrain from heavy petting, oral sex, and the like, then you are missing the whole point. If it's *love* you want, then developing *that* must come first, with sex out of the picture for awhile. And don't kid yourself into thinking that other forms of sexual activity, outside of full-on intercourse, are somehow different than "going all the way". They aren't. You can still bond emotionally through these forms of sexual activity and, frankly, men don't see a difference; therefore, the benefit of him seeing you as someone who is virtuous and intent on taking care of yourself would be lost.

In this chapter we will discuss the various forms of affection and how to avoid going too far with any of them, as well as how to navigate this tricky part of the dating process, and what to do if he might be sleeping with someone else. Restricting yourself from being physical to this degree may seem extreme, but just keep reminding yourself that it really is only temporary and it's for a great cause.

The Definition of Foreplay

The definition of "foreplay" is "Sexual stimulation preceding sexual intercourse" ...so ask yourself, "If I'm not planning on having intercourse, why am I preparing myself for it?" You are putting a lot of unnecessary pressure on yourself, and on him, and you're setting yourself up to fail. I realize you're hot to trot, it's been a long time, and he's so very sexy... but remember your goal. You are in the midst of "foundation-building-time" and you do not want sex to get in the way of that! You want him to fall deeply in love with you. You want to get to know the real man sitting in front of you—his mind, heart, soul, dreams, quirks, and you want him to get to know the real you. So snap out of it, get a grip (of *yourself*!) and stay focused!

Delaying Gratification

In today's world everything is about instant gratification—we are not used to taking our time, being patient, and waiting for things to develop slowly. However difficult it may be, we all possess the ability to put off obtaining something in order to obtain something even better. This is also called "impulse control" or "will power"—and yet, if you follow the instructions in this book you will never feel deprived or as if you are missing out on something of great value. In fact, the exact opposite will be true: *you will feel so elated, excited, and passionate about the fact that you are in control and in the process of creating something far more valuable* than a short-lived, brief sexual encounter (or series of encounters). Knowing that you have the power and that you are in the driver's seat, creating and building a love that will serve you the rest of your life—it doesn't get any better than that! So instead of moping around, feeling sexually deprived and as if you must summon up great self-restraint—remind yourself that you are only *delaying* sexual gratification and get excited about the process and the end result!

Attitude and Mind-Set

I cannot stress enough the attitude and mind-set that you need to have throughout this process. If you walk around with a doom and gloom attitude, thinking that you are being deprived of something that you desperately want, then you will be miserable and you will not be attractive to men. If this is where you are at mentally, then you need to spend some time soul-searching and decide what is most important to you and how you really want to approach your dating situations. My message is that if it's love you want, then you need to put sex on the back burner until a foundation is built (of love, commitment, mutual goals established), and if you are convinced of the same by the time you finish reading the book, then you should start to feel incredibly *excited* about putting these principles into practice. You should be *confident*, with your head held high, feeling in *control, vibrant, joyful*. Men will sense this and be even more attracted to you than ever before. You will feel *free* because you know you are no longer confused about how relationships work, or about how to avoid getting sucked into a dead-end relationship. You finally have all the information you need to build the kind of love you've always dreamed about!

What if he decides to get sex from someone else?

The fact is, he might be seeing someone else if you don't have a commitment to be exclusive. He might actively seek out someone to have sex with because you won't. My question to you is, so what? Are you afraid that he will dump you for her? If he would do that, would you really want him anyway? Truthfully, if you are following the suggestions in this book and he is continuing to pursue you even after you have had the Pow-wow, then no one else is going to win him over as a result of saying *yes* to sex. In fact, I can almost guarantee you that he will lose interest in her eventually and his feelings for you will continue to grow. He may stay with the one who is giving him sex for a time, but eventually it won't last. He will not give up on you, unless sex was all he wanted in the first place (or he knew early on that you just weren't right for him). Of course you would prefer that he not be with anyone else sexually. But are you going to go against your own values and promises to yourself in order to try to prevent that from happening? The answer should be a resounding *No!* What he does with someone else, when you are not committed to each other, is really not your problem or concern. You are moving forward, steady and clear, and it is up to him as to whether or not he wants to take care of business elsewhere, or wait for you to be ready.

Unfortunately, there are plenty of women who don't yet know these concepts and are more than willing to give it away without love or commitment, but that's not your problem. If you are not willing to put yourself in a vulnerable position to potentially be emotionally devastated, then you will be fine! If he wants to, he can date other women or even

Chapter 5 How Far Can You Go?

sleep with other women. As long as *you* aren't sleeping with him, you are in control of yourself and your emotions and you have the upper hand. If he hasn't "had you" then he will continue to be obsessed with trying to get you, and so he will not lose interest.

Maybe you won't continue to be interested in him if he chooses to sleep with someone else—that's up to you. Pamela, 37, started dating John, 42, when they met at a friend's party. The chemistry was intense and John made a sexual advance on the second date. Pamela had a brief version of the Pow-wow (she just said she wasn't ready and that she takes that part of a relationship slowly) and John said he respected her for it and wanted to continue seeing her. However, after a few more dates Pamela discovered that John was seeing someone else, sexually. She confronted him about it and he said, "I've been seeing this woman for awhile, and yes, it is a sexual relationship. But I'm not in love with her and I have told her that we aren't exclusive. We have a casual relationship. In fact, I told her I think I'm falling in love with you." Pamela told John she wasn't particularly interested in seeing someone who was sleeping with someone else, but she was okay with spending time with him as "friends". She didn't feel she had the right to insist that he stop seeing this other person, but she also felt grateful that she didn't sleep with him only to discover he was sleeping with someone else. As long as she wasn't vulnerable emotionally as a result of having sex with John, she felt in control and fine with just being friends and getting together occasionally for dinner or drinks. It didn't take long before John ended his sexual liaison and asked Pamela to be his exclusive girlfriend.

Pamela was confident enough in herself to know that if John was truly interested in her he would continue to pursue her and that eventually he would want to be with only her. She "set her standard" with John by making it clear that she would only be available for a real relationship (sexual exclusivity and commitment, based on love) and he would have to step up to the plate if he wanted her. She was patient and cool about it and it paid off. She could have flipped out and demanded that he stop seeing the other woman, or she could have felt intimidated and threatened and felt the need to sleep with him to try to compete with the other woman, both of which would have been the wrong moves. Pamela played her cards right and as a result, John is madly in love.

Do Not Make Out with Him if . . .

Some guys just don't deserve any part of you. They should not have access to your luscious lips, bubble-gum tongue (thanks, John Mayer), gentle caress, soft skin, passionate energy—let alone the most intimate parts of you—and yet so many women give all of this and more to men who are unworthy. Jill, 29, for example, went to third base with a guy was still hung up on his ex. "I felt sorry for him!" she said. That's not a good reason to be intimate with someone! As I dug further, she also felt that maybe she could sway his feelings towards her if they were more intimate. But as I suspected, he couldn't get over his feelings for his ex and Jill ended up with a broken heart herself. But what I would like for you, is that you choose to be sexual with the man of your choice based on getting what you ultimately want. I'm assuming you want real love, true commitment, and in most cases, marriage. You don't want a

Chapter 5 How Far Can You Go?

watered-down version of love, and you don't want to be someone's second choice. So, if he says he's still hung up on his ex, go ahead and date him casually if you'd like, and see what happens, but do not make out with him (or sleep with him, of course). If he makes the moves, you could say, "First of all, I take things very slowly in this department, but secondly, you still have feelings for your ex-girlfriend. I would never feel comfortable with getting physical with someone who wasn't just totally into *me*."

Other reasons to not make out with the guy: he doesn't treat you like a queen, he's chronically late or flakey in general, he is rude or obnoxious (for example, being on his phone, texting or emailing constantly while he's with you), he doesn't listen to you or seem to care about what's important to you, he seems to be too much into his friends or mother or anyone other than you, he drops plans frequently, he is drunk and/or drinks too much in general, he's just not that into you, he's not attentive, he tries too hard or not enough, or he seems insincere.

Go with your instincts here. Your inner voice will be invaluable during this process. But you have to tune into your feelings and be as present and conscious as possible. You know the Truth when you hear/see/feel it. You know when a guy seems like he is full of it or if he seems sincere. Men give major clues all the time. They will mention their ex-girlfriend too many times, or tell you what their problems or hang-ups are without even realizing they are doing so. Pay careful attention! You are interviewing every guy you date, in a sense (but without grilling him with questions), and you need to gather as much material and insights as you possibly can. Who you end up with is the most important decision you will ever make, so you want to take your time and be as aware as you possibly can be when you are with him.

Various Forms of Affection

Every form of affection outside of intercourse can be considered foreplay. There are different levels of intensity, however. Holding hands, hugging, and light kissing are very mild forms of foreplay, whereas heavy petting and oral sex are more intense forms.

As you read through each form of foreplay, consider your feelings about each one. How do you want to deal with these issues in your own life?

Kissing

Kissing can be deceiving. Just as that little piece of pie looks totally harmless, we all know it's packed full of calories. I'm not saying you should never kiss, but you certainly need to consider how serious kissing really is. Once you begin kissing, a new precedent has been established and there's no turning back. Dr. Neil Clark Warren, founder of eHarmony and author of *Finding the Love of Your Life,* writes, "Each level of sexual experience is so immediately rewarding that it's nearly impossible to be satisfied by previous levels."

As I have said previously, one of the most important aspects of the dating process is getting to know the other person as deeply as possible and in as many different situations as possible. How can you effectively do this when you're obsessed with making out? As you read Chapter 9 and discover all the things you need to know about him before getting physical, you will understand why it's smart to postpone being physical for as long as possible.

I am not going to tell you that you can't kiss until x amount of time has passed. That would be pointless and each relationship is different. But I would like to caution you to take your time. Don't be afraid to say no until you are sure your feelings for each other are strong and real. If you possess strong will power, you could always engage in one big kiss early on in the dating process, just to see what kind of kisser he is and how compatible you are together, but only if you can then put on the brakes after that, by telling him that you want to slow things down. If he seems confused and gives you a hard time about giving him mixed messages, you can always say, "I really wanted to kiss you to verify that our chemistry is what it seems to be—but ultimately I believe in taking things slowly. At least we know we kiss well together!" The danger of doing this, of course, is that it's a slippery slope and it doesn't take long to go from first base to a home run, as you probably know from past experience. So only engage in a kiss or two if you know you absolutely can pull back and refrain from going forward.

Holding Hands and Light Affection

Holding hands and light affection are like vegetables. They're good for you and low in calories. Go ahead and have as much as you like, provided you don't add anything, like butter, or some of the heavier forms of affection. Just remember that he has to make the first moves. Don't ever reach for his hand or snuggle up to him initially. Let him initiate and only reciprocate if you really feel it.

Love Before Sex

Cuddling

Most people like to cuddle. And cuddling is fine as long as you're prepared to deal with the potential hazards. Very few people cuddle without kissing, and we all know that leads very quickly to other things. I've also found that women can cuddle for a lot longer than men without anything else ever happening. We just enjoy cuddling and being close. Men, however, usually see it as a prelude to something more. So I would keep this at a minimum and you may have to have another Pow-Wow, depending on how things go.

Oral Sex and Petting

Unless you want to have sex, don't engage in oral sex or petting. Couples who go this far typically end up going all the way. Margie, 54, decided she was tired of the dead-end relationships she had had for many years after her divorce, so she said no to casual sex. But her attitude about everything else was very open. "I just figured as long as I don't have full on intercourse, it would be fine. I mean, how can I expect the guy to not be able to do anything?" But most men don't see a difference between having oral sex and having intercourse. They are both very intimate, sexual acts, in which you are naked, and touching/penetrating. What's the difference? And this is the logic that usually gets the woman to give in and go all the way. At a certain point it seems ridiculous, so you give in and do it, despite your better judgment. But if you approach the situation with confidence—knowing that you are doing the right thing, that it's okay and even imperative that you say no to all forms of sexual activity (until you've had the Pow-Wow and the feelings are established)—then you won't be led down the slippery slope.

Spending the Night Together

I know some couples who have spent the night together but didn't do anything. I also know many couples who tried not to do anything but ended up going much further than they had intended. It's very risky. The final decision is up to you as to how far you are willing to go. But you may want to follow this rule: *If you don't want to have sex, or something equally as intimate, don't allow him in your bed (or you in his)!*

Sexting, Etc.

It's a new world and everyone is texting/emailing/Skyping, and the like. This can enhance your relationship and make it more fun. It can also create problems. First of all, you don't want to be too available all the time. A little mystery is good and he needs to miss you and long for you. He can't experience that if you are available at the drop of a text. It's fine to respond to his texts and emails but keep it light, and definitely do not get into heavy sexual innuendos and banter through these forms of social media. It simply won't serve you well, and it gives off the wrong message. You want to be seen as a classy woman who carries herself with dignity. Don't get me wrong: once you are in love and committed, feel free to be wild and crazy and have fun. But in the beginning of the romance, play it cool and keep it light. If he attempts to send you a racy text pre-sex/commitment, simply ignore it at first. If he asks about it, say something like, "I'm sorry I didn't respond but it just seems a bit premature for us to be having those kinds of conversations. I guess I'm an old fashioned kind of girl, but I reserve that kind of banter for the man I love and who loves me." He needs to know that you don't just engage in sexual talk with just anyone. It is a special experience for someone worthy of that level of intimacy. That response will shut him down quickly, but if he's serious about you it won't scare him away. Instead, he will appreciate your candor.

How to Say No to Kissing and Other Forms of Affection

When your date attempts to kiss you and you're not interested in participating, simply put your hand on his shoulder, pull away a little, and say, "Please don't take this personally, but I don't feel comfortable kissing this early in our relationship. I'd rather take it slow and just get to know you better." Or turn your head so that his kiss falls on your cheek, which is a great way to give him the message without being too blunt. Giving him a kiss on the cheek is also acceptable. He may frown, but he won't feel as slighted as if you push him away without any explanation or reassurance that it's not personal.

Giving him a short hug good-bye is also a warm way of saying good-night. If he's a nice guy, he will be polite and accept your feelings. He may even feel relieved not to be under pressure to sexually pursue you. Doug, 47, had this to say. "Sometimes, as a guy, I feel so much pressure to make the moves sexually. And I've had a lot of women be the aggressors. It's fine, after you get to that point, but in the beginning I'd like to take my time because I want to get to the know the girl first. There's so much expectation

Chapter 5 How Far Can You Go?

that the guy be sexually aggressive that it's a turn-off to me sometimes."

Unlike Doug, some men may be hurt or slightly offended, but don't worry about that. If you're honest, sincere, and kind, any decent man will respect your wishes. If he gives you a hard time, then you may want to reconsider your interest in him. But don't just automatically dismiss him if he persists sexually. Even the nicest guys find it extremely difficult to reconcile the testosterone running through their veins. It's a powerful hormone that can drive men crazy—then when you add a beautiful, sexy woman to the mix, it's tough on a guy! Be understanding and compassionate, but firm in your resolve.

If you don't feel comfortable with any form of affection early on in the relationship, you could say, "Please don't be offended, but I'd rather not be affectionate until we know each other a little better. I really like you, but I move slowly when it comes to being physical. I don't want to get too distracted from getting to know you."

If he says something like, "Gee, I'm only wanting to hold your hand!" then just tell him you realize it's no big deal, but you just aren't comfortable with it right now. It's not that you're not a physical person, you just don't jump into these things so easily." You may have to be a broken record and just keep repeating yourself (patiently and warmly) until it sinks in fully.

After you have been dating awhile, he may invite you over to watch a movie. If you feel brave and decide to go, you will need some strong comebacks for any potential advances. You are already armed with many responses from the previous chapter, but in terms of making out/foreplay, try these:

He may suggest that you lie on the floor with him or on the couch. Simply say, "If you don't mind, I'd rather sit over here. I just don't feel comfortable cuddling at this point in our friendship (or relationship)." If he persists or tries to convince you that it's harmless, just keep saying, "I'd really rather not, I'm just not comfortable with it." Eventually he'll give up. Remember, you can always leave. He needs to know that you mean what you say. Don't let his pouting or irritability sway you. Men will use these childish tactics to get you to cave in, but you're smarter than that. Again, don't be afraid to lose him, or to say, "Maybe you should go home now—this isn't going well." Or, "I really like you, but all of this sexual pressure is stressful and detracts from us getting to know each other. It would be so nice if you could get a hold of yourself (no pun intended!)." It's always good to have a good sense of humor!

If you've made it as far as heavy petting, you should have said no a long time ago. But it's never too late to start over. You can say, "This has gone too far. As much as I'm enjoying this, I know it isn't right for me. Not now anyway. I'd like to stop all of this, including kissing so much, and just develop other aspects of our relationship more." This is where your self-discipline has to take over because putting all physical contact on the back burner will be more difficult than ever.

Emotional Pain

As harmless as "making out" may seem, it can bring you tremendous frustration, pain, and unhappiness. Wanda, 27, said, "I made myself crazy when I dated Kyle. I told him that premarital sex was out of the question, which he

Chapter 5 How Far Can You Go?

accepted. Part of the reason he accepted so easily was because he planned on doing everything except intercourse! He preferred going all the way, but heavy petting and oral sex was the next best thing. I went along with this for awhile because I'm very sexual too and I also didn't want to lose him. I thought I had to do *something* to keep him interested. But every time we got into a heavy make-out session, I began to feel remorseful. Even though I was participating, I really didn't want that! The fact that I was allowing it in my life brought me a lot of unhappiness. And frankly, by engaging in foreplay, our relationship wasn't at all strengthened."

BEATRICE, 36, told me, "As I look back on my relationship with Todd, I'm amazed I was even able to focus on anything other than our relationship. I was consumed with fear and self-doubt because, on one hand, I absolutely did not want to engage in heavy foreplay but, on the other hand, I really wanted to be with him. We were obsessed with each other sexually. We had already gone all the way once, but we made a promise to stop. But we couldn't stop making out, nor did we really want to. If only we could have just kissed and held each other, without going any further! Maybe if it hadn't been so good between us, I would have had more resolve. But I just didn't have the power."

At a certain point all of this behavior becomes ridiculous. You're a grown woman and you do have the power to control yourself. The key is your motivation. How badly do you want the relationship of your dreams? How badly do you want the man of your choice to love you deeply and forever? Make your decision as to how you're going to conduct yourself throughout this relationship, and then keep your eye on the prize. Avoid heavy make-

Love Before Sex

out sessions, for awhile, in order to take care of the more important business at hand: *getting to know him!*

Diverting Your Attention

A large part of abstaining is simply about diverting your attention and keeping yourself busy with other things. There are so many things you can do, and as silly as some of these may seem, they are great ways to get out and have some fun and to see the man you are dating in new ways. When my husband and I were dating and the chemistry was through the roof, we tried to avoid laying around either of our apartments. One day he mentioned that he had never been on a roller coaster before and so I said, "Come on! Let's go to Magic Mountain!" We jumped in the car and off we went, and we had a great time going on every ride there. It is something Michael still tells friends about to this day. So, be creative and fun. Think about new and exciting ways to spend your time. Here are a few suggestions:

- Have a picnic
- Throw a party or invite a couple of friends over for game night
- Get tickets to a concert, play, opera, etc.
- Try a new restaurant each week or month
- Make a list of movies you want to go see and commit to seeing one each week (no videos at home in the early stages!)
- Take a class together (foreign language, art, photography, history, public speaking, etc.)
- Go to a jazz club
- Go for a walk, hike, or ride in the car

Chapter 5 How Far Can You Go?

- Go to the gym
- Go shopping
- Go fishing and/or target shooting
- Go to a car show
- Go to art galleries/exhibits

The Three C's: Commitment, Confidence and Consistency

If you are serious about putting love before sex, then you'll want to incorporate the Three C's into your life. The *commitment* to abstain is not only about not having sex—it's a commitment to care for your body and to treat it lovingly. It's a commitment to your mind, to keep it clear and healthy. You are making a commitment to yourself, and to your goal of creating the best relationship you can create. When you are truly committed to this process there is absolutely no room for negotiation. To be successful requires this level of commitment.

Obviously, to maintain this kind of commitment you have to have *confidence* in yourself and your decision. You need to have a firm belief that what you are doing is absolutely right. You will gain this confidence as you become clearer about your reasons for abstaining and as you become more intent on achieving your goals.

Ralph Waldo Emerson wrote, "That which we persist in doing becomes easier for us to do; not that the nature of the thing itself is changed, but that our power to do so is increased." In other words, the more consistent you are, the easier it will get. *Consistency* will come as a result of your deep commitment and the confidence you have in yourself and in your decision.

Love Before Sex

There will always be times when you will feel like tearing your hair out because of your desire to be sexual. You literally have to train yourself to just feel the feelings and then redirect your energies elsewhere. Your dream relationship will be your focus and you should be so busy getting to know this man, having fun with him, and determining if he's right for you, that you don't have time to just sit around and stress out about your lack of sexual activity. You can do this!

Chapter 6
But I'm so *Randy!* What's a Girl to Do?

I realize that hormones are powerful and you're a healthy, sexual being. But what is your primary goal? To get laid? Or, is it to have the man of your choice fall head-over-heels in love with you? Remember, you have the rest of your life to have hot sex with your man, who loves you beyond words. Always keep in mind that this is a *temporary* situation. You are building something of great value and you cannot allow sex to get in the way of its development! The women who give in because they get swept away in the heat of the moment usually end up regretting it. It isn't worth it! You have to make a solemn commitment to yourself that you won't give in, no matter what, no matter how sexy he is or how hot and heavy the moment gets—you make this decision now, while you are alone and in full control of yourself and your emotions, and then you never waver from it, no matter what.

In this chapter you will find helpful tips on how to cope with raging hormones, or whatever might be leading you to stray from your decision to put love before sex. There are lots of reasons why women resist this message and we will cover those as well.

The 10 Most Common Excuses Women Use to Give in Too Soon

Getting the most out of this section has a lot to do with being honest with yourself. You will want to spend some quality time with yourself and do some soul-searching. Ask yourself if any of these points are true and do they really apply to you? You may not have been conscious of certain facts, but now that I am bringing them to your attention, maybe some of these points will ring true for you. It's all about being honest with yourself so that you can get into the solution and make your life work for you. Lots of women blame the mediocrity or demise of their relationships on the guy, but I guarantee you that you played a part as well. Having sex too soon is the most common problem, and the following are the 10 most common reasons/excuses women give for having sex too soon:

1) **It's better than being alone:** I know it's hard to be alone and if that aloneness continues for a long period of time, then it is almost unbearable. But it's imperative that you become okay with being alone. Otherwise you will be too susceptible to taking on the first guy who comes along and gives you attention. You want to "act as if" lots of men would want you and they would be lucky to have you. Carry yourself that way—if you believe it, others will too. No one wants to be lonely and Friday nights spent alone can be sad…but if you are taking care of yourself, making yourself attractive to men, and following the guidelines in this book, you will not be alone for long. Hang in there, but don't give up before the miracle happens.

Chapter 6 But I'm So Randy! What's a Girl to Do?

2) *I don't want to scare him away:* He should be concerned that his behavior could scare *you* away! The guy you want to spend your life with must want you with all his heart and soul. He has to be willing to walk through fire for you. If a guy is scared away because you want to take things slow and not have sex with him early in the dating process, then he is not the right guy for you. Remember, when you say no to casual sex the guy making the moves is forced to consider how he really feels about you. He has to take you seriously. He has to ask himself the question, "Is there potential with this girl?" He has to do some soul-searching and evaluating. If his answer ends up being, "Nope. Sorry. Can't wait. Must have sex now or I'll walk away from you" then doesn't it seem pretty clear that he wasn't a keeper anyway?

3) *I don't want to seem like I'm rushing things or playing games:* How can you be seen as rushing something when you are saying you don't know how you feel about the person yet (and vice versa) and you want to take things slow and get to know them better? You are not saying, "I refuse to have sex with you right now, unless you will commit to me and then I will immediately tear off my clothes." You aren't saying no to sex as a manipulation. You truly want to take things slow and get to know the person and have him get to know you, without sex confusing the matter. You are saying that commitment/feelings of love are pre-requisites, but it isn't a quid pro quo situation. This is the *opposite* of playing games—it is being more upfront and honest than most men ever experience in the dating world.

4) *I may not find someone better so I'm willing to settle:* You may not consciously admit that this is what you're thinking, but lots of women do, so check in with yourself and see if it isn't true for you. This book is about setting your sights high and not settling for anything less than what you truly want. You never want to settle, nor do you ever need to settle. The fact that you have these tools means you now qualify for the best men out there! They are the ones who want a woman who understands these principles and who applies them (even if they aren't able to articulate that).

5)   ***I'm not getting any younger:*** See the comments above, in #4. It doesn't matter what your age is—and you would be surprised at how many women in their fifties and sixties attended my seminars and told me that they had never had a man be deeply in love with them. They were still having sex too soon and making all the mistakes that prevent love from developing! It's never too late to learn and apply these principles. And having sex too soon never gets you what you want, unless it was only sex you were after.

6)   ***I know he won't go for it (if I set this standard and insist on the Pow-wow points):*** How do you know that? This is your not-so-stellar self-esteem talking and you need to shut her down! Remember, if he doesn't go for it then he isn't a keeper and it has nothing to do with your worthiness or attractiveness. If he rejects you and your standards it could be due to many factors: he met someone else he clicks with more than you; timing is off for him due to a recent breakup or divorce; the chemistry isn't there or he just can't envision a future with you. Whatever it is, it's okay because at least you didn't get emotionally bonded to this guy only to be potentially dumped down the road! You just move on and feel good about the fact that you didn't give all of yourself. But I have to say, most men will go for it and you just have to trust me on

Chapter 6 But I'm So Randy! What's a Girl to Do?

that—go out and practice this for 6 months. Date as many men as you can and apply the principles to the letter and let me know what happens. It does take practice and you'll make mistakes (just don't have sex too soon!), but you'll get it down and it will pay off.

7) **I prefer to let romance unfold naturally rather than try to control it and be so calculating:** And how is that working for you so far? This is what most women do and they wonder why they go from one relationship to the next without it ever working out. You can still be romantic and go with the flow and not be overly controlling...we are only talking about not having sex too soon. You are allowing the relationship to unfold naturally, you are sitting back and allowing him to pursue you and make all the moves. You are having a great time, being light and fun and yes, even romantic. But you have sexual standards and you set them. You don't allow yourself to be swept away by fantasy—you live in the real world and you ultimately want a real relationship—one that is based on a solid, sound foundation. You can't lose your sense of judgment for some hot romance that could only last one night. It is all about balance.

8) **I want to see what he is like sexually early on so I know if we are compatible**: I realize the importance of this, but what I have observed is that people who click on other levels initially, in terms of how they sound, look, move, dress, think, and so on, and who truly enjoy each other's company, are usually sexually compatible. I also know of couples who, despite having sex early on and *not* being very sexually compatible, chose to continue seeing each other anyway (and even got married, in some cases). So sexual compatibility is not something that makes or breaks a relationship in many cases. As you date and you engage in some light kissing, holding hands, and talking, you can determine sexual compatibility, without having to have sex too early in the relationship.

9) **If it's meant to be or he really wants me, then having sex isn't going to change that:** This is a nice notion but based on my observations and experiences it simply isn't true most of the time. Of course there are exceptions, as I've mentioned before, but it is not the norm. Having sex too soon can be the sole (or at least primary) reason for a relationship to abruptly end. Undoubtedly this has happened to you or someone you know. You meet someone great, you think it's going along fabulously, you have sex, and then everything gets weird. He pulls away or doesn't call again (or perhaps *you* are the one who loses interest). Or the relationship continues for a time but he doesn't treat you as well as you'd like, or it just doesn't progress well. I am not saying it always turns out this way, but having sex too soon does tend to have negative repercussions. If you want to get married and have a solid foundation for your marriage, then you will want to take this message seriously and not take a chance that sex before love won't ruin everything (or at least dilute it).

10) **I couldn't help myself—he swept me off my feet!:** This may have happened in your past, but that doesn't mean it has to happen again. You are stronger than that and you have the ability to remain in control. You just have to study this book carefully, memorize your Pre-sex Pow-Wow, make your decision now and vow you will stick to it. Most importantly, you will want to get excited about the kind of

Chapter 6 But I'm So Randy! What's a Girl to Do?

relationship you are going to build. Keeping your thoughts focused on the bigger goal and what you are ultimately trying to accomplish will help to keep you on task. You may have to look yourself in the mirror before every date and have your own personal Pow-Wow with yourself, but whatever it takes!

How to Avoid Sex Before Love

The following is a list of ideas/actions that can help you stay true to yourself. These points may be very simple but they are profound.

1) Keep your eye on the prize. You are delaying gratification for a greater goal.

2) Remind yourself prior to each date what your goals are, and give yourself a pep talk before you meet him.

3) Memorize your Responses to his advances.

4) Keep a Journal and use it to express your emotions and keep track of your progress.

5) Cold showers can be helpful!

6) Self-gratification is not a bad thing.

7) Do not be alone for long periods of time with him at his place, yours, someone else's, a car, etc.

8) Do not engage in sexual talk with him (why get both of you all worked up and send mixed messages?) If he gets too personal too soon, say, "You know, this is a pretty intimate topic! I think we should save it for later, if we are still seeing each other…"

9) Channel your energy into exercise and imagine how fabulous you're going to look when you do finally get naked with him!

Love Before Sex

10) Rather than fantasizing about having sex (which you can't have right now), visualize the relationship/marriage you want to create.

11) If it becomes obvious that he is all about sex by constantly making sexual innuendos and remarks about your body, etc... nip it in the bud (no pun intended) by setting a strong boundary, or end the relationship and move on. To set a boundary you could say something like, "I notice you're really focused on me sexually...I am more interested in us getting to know each other right now, non-sexually. Do you think you could shift your focus and just focus on getting to know me?"

12) Get out and be socially active—be everywhere, doing everything.

13) Do not drink too much on dates—you need to stay in control of yourself, and there is nothing more unattractive than a drunken woman.

14) Do not tell your friends, family, co-workers, or anyone else about your true feelings for him—it could get out and sabotage everything.

15) Make your early dating days be about having fun and being playful (vs. just jumping in the sack right away)... enjoy light forms of affection, knowing there will be so much more to explore *down the road....*

16) Get out of yourself and into some kind of service work/volunteer work. You don't want to be obsessed with the relationship.

17) Work on inner/spiritual development—learn to meditate, see a relationship coach or clinical psychologist in order to clear out any cobwebs.

18) Create a Vision Board with all of your dreams/goals laid out to inspire you.

19) Ask yourself, "How many more failed relationships do I want?"

I know plenty of highly sexual people (men and women) who were able to refrain from sexual activity during the early dating process. It may not be easy but it is definitely doable. But what if you've already gone too far? That's the subject of the following chapter.

Chapter 7
Starting Over if You've Already Gone Too Far

It is obviously easier to abstain from sex too soon if you made your decision *prior* to being in a relationship. Hopefully you will read this book and have everything in place (your Pre-sex Pow-Wow spiel, for example) and then when you're confronted with a sexual advance you know what to do and you have prepared yourself emotionally and mentally for the moment. But maybe you just bought this book and you've already gone too far and want to know what to do. Maybe you read the book but still went farther than you planned. It happens. Don't automatically assume that you've just destroyed your chances of success, and certainly don't beat yourself up. There's no room for shame in your life—you are human, after all!

It is ironic that so many women are afraid that by *not* having sex early on they will lose the guy—and yet the exact opposite is true: if you *have* sex too soon (or go too far in general), you will probably lose the guy. However, if the guy sticks around, but you know you made a mistake and you want to start over, it is possible to salvage something that might have otherwise died. *The key is that he has to be interested enough to continue pursuing you.* If he continues to call, then you have a shot. Then why bother starting over and stop having sex, you might ask? Because sex too soon doesn't just destroy relationships...it can also make them mediocre. Sex too soon creates those "few weeks, few months, or few years stands" that I talked about earlier. *You may be in a relationship but not the kind in which he's over the moon, head over heels in love, wanting to marry you right now because he loves you so much type of relationship.* That type of relationship comes when you put *love before sex.* So you want to start over and have your Pow-Wow, even though you've had sex before. And exactly how you go about doing that is what you will find in this chapter.

Ending a Sexual Relationship and Starting Over

Breaking up is painful. You gave a lot of yourself and had high hopes for this person and now that you've become emotionally attached and he's pulled away, or you have to end the relationship, it can be extremely painful. It's important to feel the feelings and experience the grieving that comes with a broken heart, and yet it's also important to move through that and on to feeling excitement and passion for the next one. Allow yourself time to heal, but there's no need to wallow for a long period of time. Because you now have the tools you need you should be able to approach dating with a whole new sense of confidence. But first, how do you break it off, or at least end the sex? The conversation should sound something like this:

"I care about you very much, but it seems like I may not be the right woman for you. I should have insisted we talk about relationship goals and where you saw this going from the beginning, but I didn't. I assumed that we were

Chapter 7 Starting Over if You've Already Gone Too Far

on the same page—that we both wanted this relationship to progress—from falling in love to ultimately getting married. I don't like the idea of giving an ultimatum because I don't want to pressure you to do something you don't seem to naturally want to do. But I do feel the need to pull away and make myself available to meet someone who does want the same things I want, and who wants them with me. I don't want to hurt you but I need to think about my future. I want something serious and real, and it doesn't seem to be happening here. Maybe we can be friends, but at this point we can't be in a sexual relationship."

Another way to put it:

"I really care about you, but I've come to the conclusion that I don't feel comfortable being in a sexual relationship. I would like to continue seeing you but only if we can do so without sex. I have decided that I am going to wait until I'm (committed and in love, engaged, or married—you choose, and do so before you have the conversation) before I get sexually involved again. It has nothing to do with you; it only has to do with how I feel. I'm just not happy this way and so I'm making a change. I hope you can accept this because it is very important to me."

Obviously use your own words and style of communicating but don't be wishy-washy. Doing this is not the easiest thing in the world to do. You are basically ending the relationship, although there is a chance that he will say, "Don't go. I love you and want the same things you do." But he may not say it right away, or ever. So after you have this spiel you have to *leave immediately*. It is awkward to stay, and hanging around makes it look like you are waiting for him to say all the right things. You have to leave with an air of confidence in order to let him know that you mean business and that you've made up your mind. You're not messing around any longer. The tone is kind but firm. There will undoubtedly be some sadness, but be careful to not exude any sense that you're devastated. If you don't think you can hold it together then hold off on having the conversation. The message needs to be "I care about you and wish it had worked out, but I'm strong and know who I am and what I want, and I'm moving on. Bye-bye!" You may be dying inside, but you never let him know that. You are calm, cool, and collected.

Another reason for leaving immediately is that a man can't chase after you unless you're *moving away from him*. In fact, you need to be moving away a lot in general with a man so that he always feels like he can't quite get enough of you. He has to miss you, have time to think about you and want you to be with him. If you're already always with him, then he never gets to miss you!

What you are doing by having this conversation, is you are 1) sharing your true feelings, so that he knows exactly where you are coming from, 2) putting him in a position where he must re-evaluate whether or not he is willing to step up to the plate (he didn't have to before because he was getting what he wanted without having to give you what you wanted), and 3) you are doing this without pressuring him to commit to you.

That's the brilliance of this approach, versus other approaches, such as saying, "Hey, I'm not getting any younger here. We either get married by June or I'm out of here!" Ultimatums can work but they don't ultimately give

Chapter 7 Starting Over if You've Already Gone Too Far

you what you want. They can demand action but it is most likely against the guy's will. Do you really want him to commit under those conditions? Don't you want this to be his idea?

Trust me; you want him to be so madly in love with you that he would never want to lose you. If he's not there then you have to start all over and that begins with *stopping the sex and walking away from the relationship.* Then you see if he pursues you. If he doesn't, then it's over. If he does, then you have potential, if you follow everything in this book. At that point you treat it as though it is an entirely new relationship with a new set of rules, based on the concepts in this book. Do it correctly from the beginning and you won't have to go through all of this starting over business, which is very challenging and it often doesn't go this way!

Also, when you have this type of conversation with the guy, it taps into that human trait we all have of wanting that which we can't have. Even though he was just taking you for granted 30 minutes ago, he might now be saying, "But I don't want you to go—I love you!" You switched things up on him and it can be confusing to a man. You are saying things like, "Maybe we can be friends" (guys hate that word!) or "Maybe I'm not the right girl for you"—these things get a man's attention because he doesn't necessarily want to lose you and he automatically becomes more interested when you're walking away and willing to lose him. Being sexually unavailable is also the best way to capture (or recapture in this case) his interest. Even though he's already had you sexually, if he likes you enough, he will want to get you back in the sack, so you use this to your advantage. It is that sexual drive to have you that drives the relationship forward. It literally is the catalyst that pushes everything forward (along with his interest in your personality, appearance, etc.). That's why it's so crucial that you not give in too soon. You need that sexual tension and desire to help you as you pace the relationship.

He makes the moves, driven by testosterone and his desire to have you, and you respond accordingly in order to gently guide things in the right direction. If the process gets mucked up by having sex too soon or going too far with making-out, then you start over, have this conversation, and see if the relationship is salvageable. If it isn't then you simply have to move on. Do not wait by the phone, or call him. Just chalk it up to another learning experience, feel the sadness and other emotions, and then get excited about the next one and vow to do things better than before.

Does Fear Hold You Back?

Fear is probably the number one reason why women don't have these crucial conversations with men. Carrie, 28, was seeing Darren, 32. They had sex too soon and Carrie knew it immediately afterwards. "I felt this sense of doom immediately after having sex for the first time with Darren," she said. "I instinctively knew it was too soon because I felt afraid that maybe he would lose interest in me now that I gave him everything. He was really kind and loving, but having sex didn't make him want to move the relationship along and I could tell that things were different," she said. Carrie and Darren continued seeing each other exclusively, but Carrie felt as if the relationship was drifting. There were no parameters for the relationship. No structure. They cared about each other so the relationship continued, but after several months Carrie started to feel dissatisfied and concerned that the relationship would just drag on and remain mediocre. But she was afraid to confront the situation because she was afraid of losing Darren. "I don't want him to think I'm obsessed with getting married and scare him away," she said.

Carrie was afraid that sex too soon would scare him away, and then she was afraid that having a discussion about what she really wanted would scare him away. This is a lot of fear to have to live with! And it's sad for me to hear because we never need to feel fear during the dating and falling in love process—other than a little healthy fear about losing our freedom and committing to just one person. But this constant fear of losing someone is unwarranted if you know what you're doing because the guy should be so in love that you feel incredibly secure about the relationship.

When you delay sex and put love first, you don't experience these types of feelings after having sex. In fact, it is the exact opposite—you end up feeling more excited about the relationship and feelings deepen (for both parties) after consummating the relationship. Sex becomes the cherry on top, so to speak. It deepens the emotional intimacy. But when sex comes before love, it isn't uncommon to feel afraid, insecure, and unsure. This only makes sense given that there is no verbal commitment, no clear expressions of love, and no plans for the future. If you follow all of the points in this book I promise you that you will not be afraid during the dating and falling in love process—not in this way, that is.

A Word About Breaking Up

If you truly want to end the relationship with someone, don't mislead him. Come right out and tell him the truth, and then stick with your decision. I know how hard breaking up is, and how common it is to end up back together several times before the relationship actually is over. But you may know how painful it is to be strung along by a guy who just won't come out and tell you it's completely over—don't do that to someone else. If you're having trouble finding the right words, you could say, "I'm really sorry but I just don't think we are a good match. But I wish you all the best in your search for the right girl."

Separating Temporarily

If you're having a lot of problems (in addition to the fact that you had sex too soon) and yet you both want to continue in the relationship, another option is to separate temporarily, for say, thirty days (no seeing each other, no talking, etc.). It is a re-grouping period in which you can each gain clarity and inner strength. When you do get back together, you have a clean slate and it truly is like beginning a new relationship. You then apply all of the principles in this book and you will be amazed at how different the relationship will be.

How Different Types of Men Might Respond and How to React to Them

Whenever I hear women say, "Men will never put up with this in today's modern world!" I feel so frustrated, because I know that's not true. I always respond by saying, "Why don't you at least try and see?!" There are so many different types of men out there, first of all, and many of them

Chapter 7 Starting Over if You've Already Gone Too Far

would welcome meeting a woman with this approach. I hear it from men all the time. That doesn't mean men won't find it challenging to be confronted with this approach. Here are a few ways he might react:

He May Not Take You Seriously, and He will Try to Change Your Mind

Obviously, most men are going to try to get you to change your mind. Plan on that being the case. And don't resent it or cop an attitude. Men are wired differently and they will try very hard to get what they want. This is a good thing and works in your favor ultimately. But you do want him to take you seriously, and to be respectful of your standards. It may take a few "broken record" conversations, in which you just repeat yourself over and over, for him to get it. But eventually he will either have to accept it or he will be gone. But remember, even the ones who initially seem to be gone, come back! Men love a challenge and even if they go away for a few days, weeks, or months, they usually resurface, to try to win what couldn't be won.

He May Feel a Need to Distance Himself

Once a man has had sex with a woman, it's very difficult to just stop the sex. It may be difficult for you too, but it's probably easier on you because it was your idea. Not having sex any longer can bring you peace of mind (if it came before love), whereas it can bring men a lot of frustration and misery, depending on the man.

If he says he needs to have some time apart, give him the space he needs. You were walking away anyway—and you aren't asking him to marry you. He can do whatever he wants or needs to do. You are moving forward and feeling good about it. Don't panic and think that you have to do something about his feelings. He will work it out and, most of the time, he will come to terms with the situation. If his feelings are strong for you, he'll come back and you can then have the Pow-Wow with him. Let him pout—it will add to his growth!

He May Express Confusion

Since sex usually affects men differently, it only makes sense that they won't fully understand your reasons for wanting to abstain for so long. They may be confused about what to do. They don't know what to think. The best way to deal with this problem is to honestly express your feelings and reasons for wanting to wait. If he still acts confused, don't let him use this as a technique to try to change your mind. After awhile, his understanding isn't your concern. You will most likely have to go over the Pow-Wow points again and again:

> *"It's important for me to take things slowly as it relates to getting involved sexually because I want a relationship that is based on a solid foundation. I want to really get to know you and I want to see if there is true potential here. I want to be in love and in a committed, monogamous relationship with the person I'm sexually involved with."*

It's very simple, and yet men find it so difficult to grasp. Part of the reason why is because they aren't used to women behaving in this way and so it really throws them off. Even if a few women have tried to take things slowly in the beginning, men can often talk them out of their position rather quickly, so for a man to meet a woman who really

Chapter 7 Starting Over if You've Already Gone Too Far

sticks to her guns, it is a bit disconcerting and strange. So don't be surprised if he expresses major confusion. Just reassure him that you mean what you say and let him grapple with it himself.

He May Feel You Are Playing Games with Him

You will want to make it very clear that your reason for making this change is to feel good about yourself. You are not giving him an ultimatum, nor are you trying to put some voodoo hex on him—you are simply not comfortable being in a sexual relationship with him any longer. Why not? Because your needs are not being met. You do not feel sufficiently loved, nurtured, adored, and cherished. You do not have a commitment from him to be exclusive, nor is marriage on the horizon for the future. Those are the new requirements for you to be in a sexual relationship, and so until those requirements are met, you are not available sexually. He may not like these new conditions and he can be suspicious all he wants, but this is how it is. You can only reassure and explain your position so many times, and then he is going to have to either get your sincerity, and the wisdom in your position, or it's best to move on and hope that the next guy you choose has a bit more depth.

The Inconsiderate Man's Response

There are all kinds of men out there at various levels of psychological, spiritual, and emotional growth. Even the nicest guy may have trouble with your new standards in the beginning, but if he responds to you consistently in this way, then you might want to head for the door:

- He will not be concerned with your feelings.

- He will be more concerned that he won't be having sex.
- He will continue to put pressure on you (once or twice can be forgiven, but a constant barrage of sexual pressure is not cool).
- He will not listen to what you have to say; he will only try to convince you that you are wrong, silly, and immature.
- He will not be interested in finding out what *you* need in order to feel more secure.
- He will drastically distance himself from you or simply disappear with no discussion or closure.

Be sure that you are not part of the problem, however. April, 36, felt angry with John, 36, despite the fact that she was ultimately responsible. "I kept telling him my reasons for wanting to not have sex, and he said he understood. But he continued to try to get me into bed. Many times I would give in. He saw the pain I was going through and he saw how depressed I became, but he kept doing it again and again. I was mad at him for days. He could never understand why I was so angry. I told him it's like walking out in the street and getting hit by the same bus every day and each time the bus driver continues to try to convince me to walk out in front of him! After awhile, I'm going to get angry with the driver, even though it's essentially my fault for doing it!"

Iris, 57, said, "It's as though all of my words went right out the window. I told him I just couldn't continue having a sexual relationship, and yet, even as the words were coming out of my mouth, he would be all over me, trying to get sexual."

Some men actually get angry. Reina, 41, said, "When I told Jerry that I felt we had sex too soon and that I wanted to

Chapter 7 Starting Over if You've Already Gone Too Far

start over without sex, he came unglued. He accused me of being crazy and childish. He said it didn't make sense given that I'm not a virgin. I felt like all he really cared about was sex."

Acknowledge the fact that you are changing the rules and that that can be disconcerting, but also make it known that it doesn't feel good to have your feelings so easily dismissed, or even attacked. You have a right to do whatever you want with your own body, and you would hope that he cares enough about you to at least respect how you feel. Reina's response could have been:

"It doesn't matter that I'm not a virgin, or that we've been having sex. I feel differently right now, and I no longer feel comfortable being in a sexual relationship with you. If you aren't interested in starting over and putting sex on the back burner, I understand and we can say good-bye now."

The Considerate Man's Response

- He'll say he understands. The last thing he wants to do is hurt you.
- He'll let you know that your relationship is more important than sex. If you need more time, it's okay with him.
- He will wait until you are ready.
- He asks what will make you feel more comfortable or more secure.
- He will not run away just because you aren't having sex.

It is refreshing to have a man actually listen to you as you explain how you feel, and then have him lovingly tell you that he understands and wants to do whatever makes you comfortable. Now that's a guy you could marry! He's the kind of man who will be there for you when you are old and gray, or when you are ill or twenty pounds overweight. Life is too short to spend your time with men who basically don't care about your feelings.

Don't make the mistake of thinking that men will help you remain abstinent. Even though they might respect your values, if you're willing to yield, they'll usually take the opportunity to have sex. Accept this and take full responsibility for your own actions.

You need to be able to recognize a good man and avoid the rest. You can get a good idea of what kind of man he is when the discussion of sex comes up. Remember, a man is much more open to discussing having a nonsexual relationship when he loves and respects you. If you don't get the response you are hoping you will get, then he will probably not be the one who will see you through your reorienting yourself to the love-first-and-sex-later way of living.

Ultimatums Don't Work

Many women, out of frustration, attempt to move the relationship along by either nagging: "When are you going to propose to me, already?!" or, by giving an ultimatum: "If you don't pop the question by next month, I'm out of here!" Nagging rarely works, and despite the fact that ultimatums can at times work, neither approach is ideal. Do you really want to get engaged under these circumstances? It seems like you are pressuring the guy to marry you, rather than it being his idea. You deserve more. You deserve a romantic proposal based on this man's undying love for

Chapter 7 Starting Over if You've Already Gone Too Far

you. You want him to be so excited about nailing the relationship with you down because he does not want to take a chance on losing you to someone else. There is no need for coercion or pressure of any kind. All you have to do is apply the concepts in these pages and trust in the process. I cover more details about getting a proposal in chapter 13.

Don't Settle!

The key point here (and throughout the book) is that you are *taking care of yourself.* You are standing up for you and you are expressing your wants and needs. You are not being needy or demanding. You are, in a very strong and clear way, drawing the line in the sand and you are making it clear that you will no longer be giving so much of yourself because what you have been giving doesn't feel right to you any longer. I realize this is scary and very difficult. You don't want to lose him. You don't want to be single again. You don't want to be lonely. But is it better to be in a frustrating, mediocre situation that isn't fulfilling for you? It isn't meeting your dreams of happily-ever-after, so why settle? You really don't have to settle. I don't care what you look like or what flaws you might possess. You do not have to settle. I don't know if this particular guy will come around and step up to the plate, but I do know that you deserve a man who will.

Consider Carmen, 42. She was seeing Joe, 52. They had been seeing each other for two years and Carmen was tired of "playing house" and wanted to get married. Joe, however, seemed perfectly content to keep things the way they were. So Carmen followed my advice, giving it her own spin.

133

Love Before Sex

She told Joe, "Joe, I love you but I don't want to be in a sexual relationship with you anymore. I would like to keep seeing you but not sexually, because I bond emotionally through sex, and it makes me want to get married. And you obviously don't want that at this point. So let's see each other but just not have sex. If you ever want to move the relationship forward, we can talk about it then, but I am not going to have sex with anyone again, until I am engaged to be married with a date set."

Needless to say, Joe was stunned and unsure of what to make of Carmen's new mandate. At first he tried to dismiss it by saying things like, "Don't be silly" and the like. But once he saw that she was serious he decided to go along with it. Undoubtedly Joe hoped that Carmen would get over this little "phase", as he saw it. But whenever he tried to make a sexual advance, Carmen had her Pre-sex Pow-Wow spiel ready to deliver. Joe made every attempt to get Carmen to change her mind, but she stood firm. Their relationship went through a period of serious tumult, but eventually Joe proposed and they set a date. Carmen got what she wanted because she stayed true to herself. She didn't feel angry, hurt, or frustrated when they were platonically dating because she wasn't giving too much of herself. She only gave what she was comfortable giving, she set her standard, and Joe finally got with the program.

Things don't always work out so well in the end, but as I see it, you have nothing to lose and everything to gain. Once you eliminate sex from the picture, negotiating a commitment is usually right around the corner.

Chapter 8
Getting a Commitment

Not all men are commitment-phobic. In fact, I believe that very few men are actually afraid of commitment. They only avoid commitment when they aren't sure of their feelings for the woman or if they feel pressured into making a commitment. Men want love and even marriage, just as women do. At times they might be a little more skittish of the idea than women are, but that doesn't mean they won't eventually commit. After all, look at how many men are married!

Unfortunately, many men will avoid commitment if they are able to have a sexual relationship without one. They have become spoiled in this regard. They know there are plenty of women out there who will engage in casual sex, therefore why make a commitment? In order to have you, though, more is required. Any man who wants you badly enough will have to give you what you need, and most will do so gladly. And besides, many men are getting tired of being able to obtain sex so easily—as old fashioned as it may sound, men do still want a virtuous woman. You don't have to be a virgin, but when you decide to get naked says a lot about you to a man, whether you like it or not. I find it amazing that so many women balk at this concept. Josie, 29, actually got angry when we discussed this. "That is such bull___! This is not the Stone Age and men who think like that are stupid!" I believe her strong emotion comes from the part of her that simply doesn't want to accept the truth... maybe because it's been difficult for her to be virtuous herself; therefore it triggers anger that is projected onto men... ? This topic taps into all kinds of painful emotions—and *shame* is usually at the top of the list. I cover this in greater detail in the chapter on self-esteem, but at this point I invite you to ponder your own past, consider other women and their experience as you have observed them, and think about the men you have known. Men don't always reveal what they really think about these subjects, but based on my own experience, as well as the interviews I conducted with men and women, men still want a woman of virtue.

Getting a Commitment

If you follow all of the guidelines in this book you will not have to be concerned with trying to get him to commit because he will practically be knocking down your door to try to get you to commit. It is never the woman's job to bring up "the relationship" and where it is going. It is always the man who should do the pursuing and moving things forward... he is the one who calls, asks out, pays, suggests future plans, makes the sexual advances, brings up being exclusive, and ultimately proposes marriage. What is your job, you might ask? Initially it is simply to be attractive, light, charming and fun. It is your job to keep him guessing and wondering about how you feel about him, and whether or not you really like him. It is your job to pace the *sexual* aspect of the relationship and set a strong boundary, which in turn establishes a strong foundation.

Chapter 8 Getting a Commitment

It is when he is extremely frustrated that he is not getting anywhere sexually that he begins to fall for you. It is not only because he is not getting any sex—but rather, it is that you are so different, unique, and challenging. It is the fact that he is getting to know the real you, non-sexually, while at the same time being driven crazy because he can't quite get all of you. It is the chase, the not being able to have you or enough of you. It is the intense feeling of wanting more and of wanting to possess you. It sets the tone and mood of the relationship. Eventually, he will be bursting out of himself, so to speak, and he will express his feelings. He will let you know that he wants you all to himself.

Many women make the mistake of thinking that they have to ask directly for what they want. And while this may be true when it comes to your career, or other aspects of your life, when it comes to the precarious and delicate early stages of dating, it can ruin everything. You do not have to ask for a commitment. Instead, you wait for him to ask you for one. The subject will come up during your Pow-Wow, but not because you are asking him to commit. You are simply telling him the conditions under which you are comfortable being in a sexual relationship—it's up to him to actually profess his feelings and make it clear that he wants you exclusively, and then you can decide what your answer will be.

This early period of the dating process reminds me of a certain type of Crane—I believe it's a Whooping Crane that does a specific mating dance. They line up, with the males and females facing each other. They do this amazing dance, but if one of the birds makes a wrong move, the partner across the aisle moves on and rejects that bird! I feel that human mating is just as sensitive—you can easily scare the other person away early on, by making a wrong move.

One of these wrong moves is letting him know how "into him" you are. It can do almost equal damage as having sex too soon. Again, it's the challenge of the chase—you become so much more valuable the more difficult it is to obtain you, whether it is sexually or emotionally. Once he starts falling for you he is going to want your heart. Your body will always be enticing to him, but that becomes less important once he loves you. When he loves you he will want all of you—your time, heart, future, companionship, *and* body.

You want to smile and be happy to see him, but he shouldn't think, "Oh boy, she is really smitten with me." Instead, you must keep him guessing as to how you really feel. This will heighten his feelings and pique his interest. He will be home, after his dates, biting his nails and scratching his head, wondering how you feel about him, "Damn, this woman!" he'll say. "I want her so badly but I have no idea how she feels about me!" It will drive him crazy, in a good way. What it eventually accomplishes is that *he will be forced to express his feelings first,* in order to get you to express yours. He wants to know if he has a chance with you. He wants to know that you feel the same way about him as he feels about you. But the primary reason he feels so strongly about you is because you have been a challenge since the beginning (physically, mentally, and emotionally) and therefore you have separated yourself from all the others. Everyone else pales in comparison now and the spotlight is on you. He is now thinking about you all the time, wondering what you're doing and who you might be with, and how he's going to get you. At some point he will blurt it out, "I love you!" Or, "I think I'm falling in love with you." He will feel compelled to express

Chapter 8 Getting a Commitment

these feelings and he will be hoping for you to express the same.

Unfortunately, the early stages of dating are tenuous and you could easily scare the other person away. Here are a few things you want to avoid saying/doing early on in the dating process:

DON'TS: Behaviors/Comments to Avoid in the Early Stages of Dating:

- ***Do Not Reveal Your True Feelings for Him (Until the time is Right).*** When is the time right? After he expresses his feelings first. And even then it's good to wait a little longer, just to keep him in suspense. This isn't playing games—it is ensuring that his feelings are real and solid before you expose your own. He could be testing you. You have to pay attention to the signs, to know that he is sincere.

- ***Don't say things like,*** *"I haven't met anyone as fabulous as you in a long time"(or any variation, such as: "I haven't felt this way about someone in awhile").* Saying these types of things make it seem like you are definitely interested, and you don't want him to know how you feel until after he reveals his feelings.

- ***Don't say things like, "Ooooh! Our first kiss!"*** Or, *"I was thinking about you a lot this week . . ." You don't want it to seem like that big of a deal.* This is a dead-give-away that you are way too excited about him, and that you have already planned the wedding.

- ***Don't say things like, "I really like you." Or, "I could really fall for you." Or, "I think I am falling for you!"*** When you say things like this you are being the giver, and you don't want to be giver. Let the sperm pursue the egg—let *him* be the one to give, even as it relates to saying sweet nothings or expressing his interest.

- **Do not gaze at him in such a way that would give him the impression that you are swooning.** The look in your eyes could be giving you away. Keep it cool. Pretend you are a world-champion poker player and you are playing in the biggest tournament of your life. He shouldn't know the cards you are holding (your feelings for him). I'm not saying that you should act so cool that he thinks maybe you *don't* like him…and you definitely want to smile and act as if you're having a good time (if you are), but he should be wondering how you really feel about him.

- **Do not refer to him as your "boyfriend" before it has been established that he is your boyfriend**. This is such a turn-off for a guy. It scares men away because they may not have decided how they feel yet, and so it makes you seem too easy or desperate. No one wants to join a club that would have them as a member.

- **Don't reach for his hand or be physically affectionate**—*let him make the first moves.* If you're physically aggressive it says you're really into him, and it is also a form of giving. Remember, you are to be *receptive*, not giving. He gives, and then you give back (always a little less).

- **Don't reveal that you have told all of your friends and/or family all about him (and don't actually tell anyone about him for awhile).** I have seen countless men scared away as a result of women spilling the beans too soon…and then when the guy finds out about it (and

Chapter 8 Getting a Commitment

they always do), they flee the scene out of fear that the woman is too smitten and planning the wedding with her friends. I know it seems irrational, but when it comes to love, men are like those Whooping Cranes. One wrong move and you're out. Although, keep in mind that this is only in the very early stages of dating. Once there is some kind of a foundation the situation isn't quite so precarious. It's one of those things where you just have to be patient and before long you will be through this phase.

- ***Do not make reference to the future, implying that you will be seeing him again.*** *For example, "I'll have to take you there sometime" or "When I see you again we'll have to do this or that..."* Again, this is being the pursuer, the giver. You want him to want to ask you out again and so you want to sit back and see if he does. You want to see if he will follow through. If you make hints about getting together in the future you sort of take that away from him—it wasn't his idea.

- ***Don't Call Him or Pursue Him in Any Way.*** Calling him is an aggressive move that will scare him away fast, unless he is really into you. There's just no reason to call him and it can be awkward. You should return his calls, but wait for a few hours (don't call him back immediately after he left the message). And don't call him back if he didn't leave a message.

- ***Don't Oversell Yourself or Try too Hard.*** All of these points, if implemented, can make you seem like you're trying too hard. It's difficult to not try too hard if you really like the guy. But try to refrain because it never works. Plus, you're the queen—you never have to try too hard.

You just have to show up and be yourself and men love you!

- **Don't be a Debbie-Downer.** This is really important. There are a lot of women who simply have bad attitudes, or are just not fun because they seem sad or down a lot. Even if your life is not what you want it to be right now, act as if it is. Don't be a drag on dates. Smile. Be radiant and effervescent. Men are attracted to joyful, happy women who are grateful for their lives. If you need to make major changes in your life in order to create more order, then do so now. Don't expect a great guy to come into your chaotic world and be willing to take that on, along with your bad attitude. You can change. Become the kind of woman that you would want if you were a man, and create the kind of life and living environment that a great guy would be comfortable in.

- ***Don't hint about, ask for directly, or demand with an ultimatum, a commitment.*** Commitment should come voluntarily, from the man, because he is so crazy about you that he wants you all to himself. Follow all of the principles in the book and he will naturally fall in love with you and he will want you exclusively. Trust the process and don't make any of these mistakes!

DOs: What to do in the Early Stages of Dating

- **Keep it light.** On dates be yourself—charming, fun, light-hearted, easy-going (but not too easy-going…a little spunk goes a long way!). Reserve your entire life story for another time, down the road when he's in love with you. Don't reveal all of your scars/wounds/trauma right off the bat. He doesn't need to know you're in AA on the first date,

Chapter 8 Getting a Commitment

does he? Why not just say you prefer to not drink and leave it at that for now? You will let him know about yourself slowly, over time, which will keep him fascinated. It can be overwhelming and scary to hear about someone's crazy family, what medications the person is taking, her ex-boyfriends from hell, and so on, all at once. You're not hiding anything, and you never lie. But you do want to take your time and let him know tid-bits about you as time unfolds. He should be curious about you and asking you questions. If he never does, then you may want to reconsider if he's the guy for you. You want a man who is interested in you and not too wrapped up in himself.

- **Be Appreciative.** Be appreciative of everything he does: "Oh, I love this restaurant—thank you for bringing me here!"…but don't act as if you are new to special treatment. Don't say, for example, "No guy has ever taken me to such a nice place before!" You want him to feel as if he has a great catch—that he would be moving *up* if he were to be lucky enough to win you over.

- **You Must Be Willing to Lose Him & He has to Sense This. Utilize the "Maybe I'm not the Right Girl for You" Tactic.** We discussed this in another chapter but I can't stress enough its importance. The guy always has to have this sense that he could easily lose you. He has to know that you will not put up with any bad behavior, and that you mean business. I don't mean in a tough way—but in a kind but firm way. He needs to think to himself, "This girl could get any guy she wants and I better stay on my toes." And if it comes right down to it, you may actually have to pull out the big guns and say, "You know, I may not be the right girl for you . . ."

- **Be Interested/Involved in Your Own Life.** This is all part of not seeming too into him, or that you are already planning the wedding. He should feel as if he can never quite get enough of you, and that you have a full life that you love.
- **Allow him to lead.** I'm not talking about being submissive or not offering your opinions, but do try to sit back and see what he does. Don't try to control every aspect of the date—see where he wants to take you, how he directs the date, and the conversation. All you really need to do is show up, be beautiful, and have fun. Your job is easy—let him do all the work, at least on the first few dates. He wants to try to impress you (or at least he should be wanting to!), so allow him that space.

5 Top Reasons Why He Won't Commit

There could be a hundred reasons why a man won't commit to you, but here are a few of the most common possibilities:

1) **He Knows You Aren't the One for Him.** He may change his mind on this later, but for now he is not convinced that he wants something serious with you. Even if you have become physical with each other, he may secretly know you aren't right for him. He may not let on that this is the case, especially if he wants to continue being sexual. If you're sure you want him, apply all of the principles in this book. If you're having sex, stop (see chapter 7). Completely start over and see if he doesn't come around. Many men do, but if he doesn't, you've got to move on. By saying no to sex you force him to honestly consider whether or not there is real potential with you, so set your

standard and then see what he does with that. Commitment is the obvious next step, and after you have been seeing each other for a time he should be able to tell if he's willing to give it his best shot. If he is clear you're not a keeper, then let him go and move on. Don't try to hang on to something that isn't meant to be. Find someone who really wants you.

2) **You Didn't Set the Right Standard at the Start of the Relationship**. If you didn't do things right from the start it's a constant battle trying to regain control. If sex occurs too soon, it's almost guaranteed that feelings will be altered, and not usually in the right direction. Getting a true commitment becomes more difficult. A strong foundation wasn't created, therefore the relationship is on shaky ground. The only solution is to start over by ending the sex and setting a new standard (see chapter 7).

3) **He is Not Sufficiently in Love**. If he is unwilling to commit, then his feelings are not deep enough. You will have to set a new standard and continue applying all of the principles in this book in order to deepen his feelings. Study chapters 10-13 to determine the areas you need to work on the most.

4) **It has Nothing to Do with You.** Some men are incapable of committing to anyone. Maybe the timing is bad for him and he won't allow himself to fall in love. Maybe he is in love with someone else—he hasn't gotten over his ex, for example. But don't use this as an excuse to not take responsibility. In most cases it's because you are either not a good match, or you didn't set the right standard from the beginning.

Love Before Sex

There is nothing more exciting than when a man starts to fall in love, and wants to move the relationship forward. It is a time of butterflies in the tummy and daydreaming all afternoon about all of the possibilities. However, do not lose your cool—you still have lots of important and serious work ahead of you! There is a lot you need to know about this man, so check out the next chapter and discover everything you need to know about him.

Chapter 9
What You Need to Know About Him Before Getting Physical

You can't be too careful about choosing a mate. What could be more important than selecting the right partner? It is literally the most important decision you will make. There are so many things to consider. This chapter will be particularly helpful for you if you don't typically pay attention to the details and if you tend to get involved with the wrong men over and over again, often missing the red flags. You will be inspired to create a Man Plan, as well as a Relationship Map. I suggest using the workbook I created to help you go through these exercises. You will find it on my website, **www.lovebeforesex.com**. By the time you're finished you will be very clear about the type of man you want to find.

Cart Before the Horse

Most people put the cart before the horse—they meet someone, and if there is an attraction, they get physical within the first few dates. It is typically *after* sex that they begin to get to know the person. This makes no sense considering that via Oxytocin you bond emotionally with the person, leaving you emotionally vulnerable to someone you don't really know.

If you are serious about meeting the right person and building something real and lasting, you will want to have your priorities straight. This isn't about being a prude or too business-like when it comes to romance. If you want to find someone to hopefully spend the rest of your life with, then who you get involved with now, physically and otherwise, is extremely important. So it only makes sense that you take your time and get to know what this guy who is pursuing you is all about. And only with sex out of the way can you maintain enough emotional and mental stability to do it right.

Getting caught up in heavy make-out sessions will only complicate the process and make it harder for you to see him clearly. Again, there's plenty of time for sex *after* love has been established. Right now the task at hand is getting to know this person, thoroughly.

The Most Important Qualities to Look for in a Mate

There is no perfect person out there, and it is difficult to generalize. However, when considering a lifetime mate, the following traits should be at the top of your list.

CHARACTER/INTEGRITY

Rather than being mostly concerned with whether or not he's tall and has a full head of hair, make good character traits your top non-negotiable aspect of a mate. Looks fade but a man's character will determine his true value. Watch closely for any bad behavior or willingness to lie or cut corners ethically. You want to know if this is a stand-up guy. Think about the kind of relationship you want and how you want to feel on a regular basis. You want to experience a sense of security knowing that you can trust this man explicitly. There is nothing more valuable in a marriage. So be watchful as to how he treats others, his level of honesty, and so on.

UNSELFISH

This is so important. If you want children (or already have them), think about the type of guy who can put his own needs aside in order to be a full partner as it relates to taking care of the children. When a man really loves a woman he cares about her so much that he wants to take care of her, and his needs take a back seat. For example, he's willing to do the things you enjoy, even if he doesn't enjoy them so much. There is nothing more attractive than an unselfish man (and nothing more unattractive than a selfish one!).

HEART

You're a lucky girl if you end up with a man with a good heart. I'm not talking about someone who is overly nice or too much of a softy—I'm talking about a man who has compassion for others, especially for women, children, and animals. Someone who cares about his family, community, country, and the planet. A man who is connected to his own emotions and who can cry at a sad scene in a movie, for example. Most importantly, someone who cares about *your* feelings and is able to address your feelings whenever the need arises. For example, if he inadvertently hurts your feelings, or notices that someone else has, he is capable of hearing you when you express your feelings and he shows concern.

NO ADDICTIONS

You obviously don't want to end up with an alcoholic or drug addict. But you'd be surprised at how often women overlook this because they don't recognize the problem. He doesn't have to be a skid-row, morning drinker to be an alcoholic. He may be a high-functioning alcoholic who is able to hold down a job, and only gets drunk occasionally (the *periodic* drinker). If he has a difficult time stopping once he starts (the *majority* of the time), and drinking causes any kind of problem in his life—for example, he misses work because he's hung over, he gets in fights with people, his relationships suffer, or he misses out on important events because of it— then this could be a sign that he has a problem, which will only get worse over time. Just be careful and don't ignore the signs. If you have a hunch that he has a problem, you will not be able to change him. He has to be able to admit he has a problem and then be willing to get help or quit on his own. The worst thing you could do is enable him to continue drinking by continuing to see him and taking care of him (lots of women do!). Sometimes the best thing you can do is let the person go so they can hit a bottom and eventually get the help they need. Make life easier on yourself—find a man who is clean/sober and not struggling with any addictions.

RELIABLE/RESPONSIBLE

This could go under the heading of character. Have you ever dated someone who was flaky? If he was terrible about being on time or returning calls promptly it had to have driven you crazy. Don't think he will change if you get married because he won't. Save yourself a lot of frustration and avoid getting involved with a man who is unreliable and irresponsible.

CONFIDENT/SECURE

We are all attracted to confidence. Confidence is sexy. But it's important for many reasons. A confident man believes in his own capabilities, feels that he is competent, and does not feel inadequate. He realizes he's not invincible and that he has limitations, but he carries himself in such a way that instills trust. You want to be able to trust that your man can follow through and accomplish things in life. You want him to believe in himself and not be overly reliant on you. You want to be able to trust his judgment and believe in him. You will respect your man if he is confident, and feeling respected is the foundation of his happiness in the relationship.

LEADERSHIP

Even if you are striving for equality in a relationship, you will want to look for a man with leadership qualities, especially if you plan to stay home while raising your children.

A leader commands respect and instills trust. If you don't feel this way about your man, there could be serious problems down the road. A woman who doesn't respect her husband eventually has contempt for him. A married male friend of mine once said, "I'm nothing more than a guest in my own house. I'm only there to take orders and serve my wife's needs." His wife obviously has a part to play in this, but he also had failed to win her respect.

A man who is a real leader takes control of his life and doesn't rely on others to run it for him (he also, however, doesn't constantly try to control you). He knows how to make decisions and stick to them. He is strong, yet fair. Some of his strongest traits are the following:

He doesn't compromise. He doesn't go against what he knows to be right. He follows his conscience. He may take others' opinions into consideration, but he makes up his own mind and doesn't compromise, especially when it comes to ethical and moral issues.

He doesn't shirk responsibilities. A leader realizes his responsibilities and fulfills them. He doesn't try to get out of them. This doesn't mean that he never struggles with responsibilities, but he doesn't hide and try to push them onto others. In most cases, he thrives on assuming responsibility. Although it can be scary for him to have overwhelming responsibilities, such as a family, he loves the feeling it gives him. He loves providing for his family and making them happy.

He doesn't allow others to dominate him. He is his own man. No one can walk all over him or tell him what to do (including you). This is not to say that he's stubborn; he is just independent and feels he is capable of solving his own problems and making his own decisions.

He has humility. As strong a leader as he might be, if he doesn't have humility, he will come across as arrogant, mean, and unfair. Humility is a very attractive quality in a man, especially the more capable and gifted he is. A humble man knows his strengths, yet also realizes his limitations. He knows he isn't perfect or invincible. He knows he needs to consult others in many situations. He knows he doesn't "own" people and that they have rights also.

He has a desire to protect women and children. With the confusion of roles today, men aren't sure if women want chivalry. But many women prefer a man who has the desire to protect. It doesn't mean you aren't equal in value or intelligence. It is a matter of appreciating the differences. It's wonderful to see a man who is concerned about the welfare of women and children, and nothing is more revolting than a man who has the attitude that they should fend for themselves. Someone told me about several couples in Los Angeles who broke up during the earthquakes because many of the women didn't like the way the men responded. Some men were just too concerned with themselves. On the other hand, I saw on the news a couple who were married after the earthquake because of one man's chivalry. He saved the woman's life, and they fell in love. If you like this quality in a man, do what you can to awaken it in him. Let him know how much you appreciate his efforts.

He is able to overcome his emotions. A leader is able to overcome his emotions *when necessary.* He doesn't allow them to rule him or destroy his confidence. This is especially necessary in the face of an emergency. I am not saying that men shouldn't express their emotions. There is nothing wrong with men crying or expressing their feelings, but a certain amount of control over their emotions is preferable.

He is hard-working. A leader is not lazy. He doesn't sleep all day, waiting for the unemployment check to arrive and then head over to Mom's just in time for dinner. He works hard, maybe even at two or three jobs in order to support his family. If he comes into hardship, he doesn't make excuses for his situation or blame it on others. He picks himself up and does what he can to fix the situation. He doesn't allow himself to be a charity case and does not want others to pity him.

He has a sense of humor. A good leader is not overly serious. He is able to laugh at life and at himself. He knows how to "lighten up" and have a good time. And yet, he also isn't the type of guy that others make fun of, or put down on any level. He commands respect.

He is not overly insecure. Some men are extremely insecure, and as a result, they can come across as very "needy." A true leader does not have this problem. If he has a bout of insecurity, he quickly overcomes it. Sometimes men who seem to have oversized egos are actually insecure underneath. They have to be "big shots" and are constantly trying to impress others because of their insecurities. A good leader knows he has flaws and weaknesses, yet he believes in himself.

A GOOD PROVIDER

Even if you are financially secure and intend to stay that way, you may want a man who is also financially secure and who sees himself as the primary provider. Most women plan to stay home at least for awhile when they have children, and therefore they need someone who will assume full responsibility of providing for the family.

He must be capable of providing the necessities of life: a roof over your head, food, medical attention when necessary, and so on. No matter what hardships may come his way, he feels responsible for being the primary provider for the family.

It's up to you to determine what level of financial security you need in order to be happy. We all come from various social classes. We all have different desires. One woman may be perfectly happy living in a small apartment with very few luxuries. Another woman may require more. There is nothing wrong with either one of these scenarios, it's really a matter of tastes and desires.

Chapter 9 What You Need to Know About Him Before Getting Physical

It is within a man's nature to want to provide for his family. This brings him tremendous joy and fulfillment. It makes him feel more manly and gives his life more meaning. He develops a healthy sense of pride and accomplishment as he takes on the huge responsibility of providing for his family.

Never look at a man simply as a paycheck, however, or as someone who is there to provide you with every little material wish. This is not his job in life. If he wants to shower you with gifts or other luxuries, that's up to him, but to *expect* it is impolite and unattractive. Also, never take him for granted. He works hard to provide you with the best life has to offer, and he needs to be appreciated for that.

The following are a few points of concern in the areas of finances. It is said that the two most common issues that lead to divorce are sex and money—so it's an area you definitely want to understand when it comes to your man.

Is he responsible with money? Watch out for men who aren't good with money. It's hard enough to be happy and make a marriage work. Obviously, not all men will be debt-free or without any money problems, but it's important that he at least be responsible in paying his bills.

Is he cheap? If you are a frugal person and you like that in a partner, then it could be a good match. But a relationship with a man who is extremely *cheap* is frustrating, to say the least. I once saw a man on a talk show who was a millionaire, and yet he would wait in the parking lot of a particular bakery for 4:00 p.m. to roll around, which was when the doughnuts went on sale! You may be able to accept someone like that—this man's wife didn't seem to have too much of a problem with it. But I think it's better to find someone with balance.

A man who is cheap can make you feel as though he doesn't care about your needs. He's more concerned with saving a buck. He denies you of certain needs and desires that are very important to you, which doesn't make you feel cherished.

Does he spend foolishly? On the flip-side of cheap is the man who spends lavishly. If he can afford it, fine. But if he can't, it spells trouble for a marriage. You have to think long-term, at least when considering him as a lifetime mate. Before you actually get married you need to know exactly what his financial situation is . . . for example, does he have a lot of debt? Notice if creditors are calling him, and find out what his credit score is. This is important information.

Is he organized and does he plan ahead? A man who is good with money has a system for managing his money and knows how to plan ahead. He doesn't have a stack of bills that just lay there for weeks or months. He looks to the future and anticipates how much he will need and when. He is thoughtful about these responsibilities, and he takes them seriously.

A GOOD FATHER

If you are looking for a lifetime mate, and you want or already have children, you will want to carefully consider what kind of father he would be. Sometimes you can get a feeling about this, but there are specific traits you can observe in him.

How does he interact with children? Try to determine if he even *likes* children. Some men are natural family men and look forward to having children, whereas other men can take them or leave them. Madeline, 43, married at 39 and desperately wanted a child. Her husband had no desire for children, but agreed to have a child because Madeline wanted one so badly. Unfortunately, Madeline ended up having to do everything for the child; her husband had little interest. This put a huge burden on her, and made child-rearing a lonely experience. If you want children, seek out a man who wants them as well and who sees himself being a big participant in being a parent.

Is he fair and just? A good father will listen to all sides and will strive to come up with solutions (with his wife) that will benefit everyone. He doesn't just "rule with an iron fist." He is open-minded and can admit when he is wrong. Look for these traits as you are dating the man in your life. If he is like this generally, then most likely he will be this way with your children.

Will he be available? A good father is available to his children. They need a father who is there, not just physically, but in spirit. He is present and engaged. It's sad to hear grown men and women say that their fathers were never around because they were too busy with their careers. They may have made a lot of money and gained a lot of prestige, but their children suffered greatly. I should mention that there are times when a family must make sacrifices—for example, when times are hard and the father needs to work two or three jobs, naturally diminishing his time with the children. This is when mom has to be even more supportive and fill in as best she can.

Is he firm? Children need this quality in a father. They won't feel secure without it, and they'll most likely turn into little terrors. They need to know that there are boundaries, and a strong father can help with this. Children need to respect their fathers. This gives them a feeling of stability and order in their lives.

Is he loving and affectionate? This is probably the most essential quality any parent can have. My uncle Garth, who has 10 children, says, "You've got to *drown* your children in love. They have to know that you adore them." Children, especially babies, need large doses of affection. When children get a little older, they don't always want their parents kissing them, but raising children with regular hugs is essential. Watch and see how demonstrative he is naturally. Is he lovable and cuddly, or is he rather cold?

Is he a good teacher? Is he the type of man who would be interested in teaching his children important principles in life, or how to function effectively in the world? Would he be willing to help them with their homework, or would he be too busy? Most men love to impart their knowledge and expertise to others, especially their children. But some men just aren't into it. Children need guidance, and unless you want to the be the sole one to give it to them, you will want to find a man who is looking forward to being a teacher to them.

Can he provide guidance? Children need to feel secure in knowing they can turn to their parents for direction. They need a father who has the answers or is willing to find the answers. When you're dating consider these issues. Think about what kind of father he would be.

Is he dependable? A good father can be trusted. His word is his bond. When he says he is going to do something, he does it. You want this quality in your mate and the father of your children.

Is he sensitive? A good father cares about his children's thoughts and feelings. He will patiently listen to them, no matter how long it takes them to express themselves. He really *cares* about what they have to say and doesn't push them away. He tries to fulfill their needs and even little requests that seem insignificant to him, but which are crucial to the child. Notice how he listens to you to get an idea of what he is like in this area.

Is he good with your children from a previous relationship/marriage? Most families are blended families. And did you know that approximately 70% of blended families end in divorce? That's pretty staggering, but not all that surprising when you consider how challenging it is to bring several people from both sides and attempt to get along. It's beyond the scope of this book to go into too much detail here, but obviously you want to make sure the new guy does well with your existing children. Take your time in introducing them, and make sure he's someone you could take seriously and see a future with—but it isn't necessary to wait too long either. This is a complicated topic, so I suggest you think deeply about it if you have children and perhaps even meet with a professional in order to work out the kinks if you're attempting to blend families.

KNOWS HOW TO TREAT A WOMAN

Ask any man if he understands women and you will undoubtedly get a puzzled look and a comment like, "What, are you *kidding*?!" There are, however, some men who instinctively know how to treat a woman. Maybe their mothers or past girlfriends taught them. If you can find a man who understands the nature of a woman, you will be making your life a thousand times easier.

Consider these qualities in judging how he'll treat you over time:

He allows you to express your feelings and emotions. I know it's rare, but I wouldn't consider marrying a man who wasn't able and willing to let me express all of my emotions to the fullest. This isn't to say that you should dump all of your emotions on the poor guy on a regular basis… it's important to utilize your girlfriends, therapist, mother, or whomever you trust and is part of your support system—but the man you marry should be able to be present with you and hear you out when you need to share your innermost thoughts and feelings. If he seems to always tune out or shut you down, or deny your feelings, or act distracted to the point where you can tell he is not interested in hearing you, then this is not the right guy for you. Trust me, you will be frustrated for life. All men have limits, and most men find women and their emotions to be a bit overwhelming, but if he loves you he will want you to share your emotions with him.

My own husband is a great example of this. He naturally has a high capacity for processing emotions, but he tells me all the time that he loves to hear me talk and if I tend to go on and on he never shuts me down or makes me feel rejected for sharing my feelings. It's an incredible trait to find in a man.

He makes you his partner. Regardless of how traditional your relationship may be, most of us want to be considered a partner in life with our mate. He may be a very strong man with strong leadership skills and a desire to be the head of the house, but it's the *attitude* of the man that

Chapter 9 What You Need to Know About Him Before Getting Physical

counts. Does he view you as his slave who is there simply to fulfill his needs, or does he view you as his lifetime partner who will be by his side and participate in decisions that will affect both you and your children?

He gives you space. You obviously lose a certain amount of freedom when you get married, and most men do want their wives to be available to them. But too much time together can get stifling for both parties. It's important to have your own space and time to yourself. Just as my husband has his annual boys' ski trip, I go on trips with friends or even alone sometimes and my husband is fine with that.

He cares about what's important to you. Every year for Christmas, my father brought home a miserable, little, scrawny tree for the house. And every year, I cried and asked why we couldn't have a big, pretty tree like everyone else. My father didn't mean to hurt me, he just wasn't clued in to how important it was for me. But small, heartfelt desires can mean the world to women, and if you can find a man who understands what's important to you and strives to give those things to you, the more cherished you will feel.

He pampers and spoils you. We all enjoy getting flowers, little gifts, cards with romantic words written on them, and other mementos of love and affection. Whether he spoils you with words, gifts, or attentiveness, it's one of the things that bring women joy and fulfillment. There are plenty of men out there who are clueless in this department so consider yourself fortunate if you find one who gets it. This kind of treatment makes a woman feel special and loved. Just remember, there is a difference between being *spoiled*, and being a *spoiled brat*. You always want to show appreciation and you want to give back in ways that are important to him.

Love Before Sex

The more a man loves you the more he will be driven to pamper you—he will feel compelled to do it. Be careful, however, not to ask for this kind of treatment. If he doesn't give it to you on his own, then either you will need to look at how you are treating him, or you will need to determine if you can accept a man who doesn't have this nature. Men will give what they want to give or what they are inspired to give. To ask for it directly diminishes the spirit of his giving. You can ask for his help in fixing things, or giving you a ride to the airport, for example, but not love/affection.

I also suggest that you don't accept expensive gifts until the relationship is very solid, and the two of you have expressed feelings of love. A man could easily get the wrong message, otherwise. If you accept his gifts, he may think you are much more serious than you might be. He also might expect you to go further sexually than you want to go, in exchange for his generosity. If you've been given an expensive gift early in the relationship, you could say something like, "Thank you so much, but I just can't accept such an expensive gift at this point in our relationship. Can we put gift giving on hold for awhile?" As difficult as this is to say, it beats feeling indebted to a man when neither of you—nor the relationship—are ready.

As you are dating, you want to feel free—free to say no when he asks you out or to date other men if you aren't committed. When money and gifts get involved too soon, the whole relationship becomes overly complicated.

He understands. You want to find a man who is compassionate and understanding. When you are down, or hurting for some reason, you want him to put his arms around you and say, "Everything is going to be all right. I'm

Chapter 9 What You Need to Know About Him Before Getting Physical

here for you." You do not, under any circumstances, want a man who is overly critical of your mistakes or any flaws you might have. He may be aware of them but he is supportive of you. He is on your side. He loves you just the way you are. Ideally, you want to find a man who finds even your little flaws and idiosyncrasies cute and adorable.

He is loving and affectionate. Most women I know love lots of affection. You will need to find a man who is compatible with you in this area. Every woman has a very deep need to know that she is loved. A man who never verbally expresses his love makes for a very cold partner. You end up feeling empty. No matter how in love you may be with the man, you will feel alone at times. It's been said that men fall in love through their eyes, and women fall in love through their ears. Women need to hear loving, tender words. We need to hear, "I love you" on a regular basis.

CREATE A *MAN PLAN* AND A *RELATIONSHIP MAP*

A *Man Plan* is simply a detailed description of the man with whom you want to spend the rest of your life. A *Relationship Map* is a detailed description of the type of relationship you want. Women often talk about the type of guy they want to marry, but they don't often consider what the relationship itself might look/feel like. Spend some quality time sketching out what you want so that you have a visual in mind, something to visualize and work toward. Don't set it in stone, however, because you could meet someone who doesn't have everything you listed and yet he could be the perfect guy for you. This is just a general guideline. Go to my website, **www.lovebeforesex.com**, to see the Workbook I created to go along with this book. In it, you will find help in creating your Man Plan and Relationship Map, and more.

YOUR MAN PLAN

The following is a list of questions to ask yourself when creating your Man Plan. Think about the kind of man you want to be with and place him in a variety of situations to determine how your ideal mate would react. For example:

- Is he supportive of your dreams/goals? Would he hold you back in any way?
- How is he with children in general? If he has children, how is he with them and in particular, when you are with them?
- How does he behave with his extended family? And yours?
- How does he treat you when you are ill?
- How does he behave when *he* is ill?
- Does he give you space, or is he controlling?
- How is he with money? How do you see the two of you dealing with money in your relationship/marriage?
- What are his political beliefs and do they gel with yours (and is that important to you)?
- Is he an affectionate/warm person, or is he more reserved?
- How does he treat others?
- Do you trust him?
- How does he deal with conflict? How do the two of you work through conflict together?
- Does he enjoy his work and is he good at it? How is he with co-workers or employees?
- Is he a generous person in general, or somewhat stingy?

Chapter 9 What You Need to Know About Him Before Getting Physical

- Is he the type of guy who considers the needs of others ahead of his own at times? Or is he quite selfish?
- What is his relationship with his mother like? How does he speak about her? And his father? Siblings?
- How does he speak about his past relationships? What clues can you glean as it relates to how he treated them?
- Is he humble? Does he come off as a know-it-all, or is he open to learn?
- Does he have a good sense of humor? Does he make you laugh? Does he laugh at your jokes?
- What are his top priorities in life? What is he most focused on?
- Has he ever been in prison/jail?
- Is he a forgiving person, or does he seem to hold grudges?
- What type of communicator is he? Is he capable of discussing feelings and processing issues in general?
- Does he run hot and cold or is he consistently loving and warm toward you?

YOUR RELATIONSHIP MAP

Take some time alone and create your Relationship Map. Think deeply about what your dream relationship actually looks like... how do you spend your time? How do you deal with extended family, friends, and your social life? Obviously it won't be set in stone. When you meet Mr. Right many things could change in ways you can't imagine now—but at least give each of these points some consideration and try to get a picture of the type of relationship you want. These questions are not for the purpose of grilling him to get the answers. You discover the answers to these questions slowly, over time, through conversation and observation.

Lifestyle. Think about the kind of lifestyle you want to share with your partner. The lifestyle he is living, blended with your own, reflects what your day-to-day life might look like, the kinds of people you will associate with, and where you will go. The kinds of places he takes you, where he lives, how he spends his vacations, and who he spends his time with are all indicators of what your life together would be like.

Religion. Is religion important to you? Do you care if it is important to him? Religious beliefs run deep for many people and being committed to someone who disagrees with your beliefs can be very frustrating and painful. Find out:

- Does he belong to a particular religion?
- How important is it to him?
- If not part of a particular religion, does he believe in God?
- Does God play a role in his life?
- Does he believe in prayer, and does he pray? How often?
- How would his beliefs affect his approach to child rearing, and how would it conflict with your beliefs?
- Is he concerned with the afterlife or is he more focused on the here and now?
- Is it important to him that you share the same religion? How do you feel about that?

Extended family. At some point you will want to meet his family and this will tell you a lot about whether or not you could build a life with this man. Although you're not marrying his family, depending on how close they all are, in a way, you are. What is his mother like? How does he feel about his mother? And his father? How close is he to his family, how does he treat them and vice versa? These are the kinds of questions you will want to ask yourself as you get to know him and his extended family. Imagine family get-togethers and holidays. Can you see the two of you meshing well together? Here are some additional questions to consider here:

- What is his family's level of influence? Is he able to make decisions without their consent or influence, for example? Are they a huge part of his life?
- Is there potential of one or more of his family members moving in with him now or in the future? Could you handle that?
- Does he have ex-wives and/or children from a previous marriage? And if so, what are the answers to the above questions?
- After having met his family members, ex-wives, and children, how well do you get along with them? Can you see yourself being able to juggle all of life's responsibilities with all parties involved, and still love your life?
- If you have children from a previous marriage, how does this new guy treat them? Do they like him?
- Do you want a traditional melding of both families, or do you want to tailor your relationship to your unique needs? Not everyone has to do it the Brady Bunch way...some families are non-traditional and keep things more separate. Blended families are complicated and so I suggest you work with a professional to determine what's right for you.

Politics. It is possible to have completely opposing views and still maintain a good relationship—however, it is typically more harmonious if you are both on the same page when it comes to political beliefs. This is primarily because your political beliefs tie in so closely with your values in general. Get to know his views and what he thinks about various world issues. Be open and receptive and don't criticize his point of view. But if you vehemently disagree you can say so, in a respectful way, and then decide if you could continue to be so diplomatic should you stay in a long term relationship with him.

Goals/Dreams. What are his dreams, and do they coincide with yours? What does he want to accomplish in life and does he have a plan for it? Watch his actions and see if he actually takes steps to make things happen, versus just being a dreamer. I've known a few women who became very disenchanted when, after years of being married to dreamers, realized that these men were big talkers and not at all ambitious. If this is important to you, then pay close attention to not only what he says, but also to what he does. Ideally you two have similar dreams that are harmonious with each other (like having a family, or building a specific business).

Communication. We all know communication is one of the most important aspects of a healthy relationship. You have to be able to talk to your partner. You want to find someone who is open, honest, forthcoming, willing to listen and also willing to talk. You need to find a way to resolve conflict, because there is conflict in every relationship. We trigger each other emotionally, and how we react to those reactions is what separates those who just continue the same unhealthy patterns over and over, and those who actually

Chapter 9 What You Need to Know About Him Before Getting Physical

learn and grow from their experiences. To help you work through conflict and create ongoing healthy communication, I highly recommend reading *Non-Violent Communication*, by Marshall Rosenberg. He points out that the key to great communication is sharing the underlying *unmet need* that is always there when feelings are hurt or negative. So, for example, if your date is chronically late, or he said something that upset you, instead of attacking and blaming by pointing the finger, you take responsibility for your own feelings (I felt hurt, angry, frustrated, etc. when I saw you do this or when you said that) and express what it was that you were *needing*...for example, understanding, consideration, loving treatment, respect, and so on. And then you can make a request. So, you might say something like, "When you are late picking me up I feel frustrated/hurt/etc. because I really need to know that you care about me and that my feelings matter to you. And I'm wondering if, in the future, you would be willing to call me if you're going to be late."

Watch how he naturally communicates and if he is able to actually process difficult emotions, as well as be present for you when you need to do so.

Affection. You probably know couples who are incompatible in this area...one of them always seems to want more affection than the other; one is a snuggler and the other isn't. Over time you'll see how he is in this department and you'll want to find someone with whom you're compatible.

Sex. Once you're in love, committed, and the future goals have been generally established, you will be sexual with this person (unless you are choosing to wait until you are engaged or married). You will see how compatible you are and hopefully it's a great match! But even if it isn't perfect, there are ways to improve the situation. You could go to a sex therapist and get tools to help you meet each others' needs. Don't give up too quickly just because the sex isn't great initially. But as you create your Relationship Map, think about what kind of sex life you want to have—frequency, style, and so on. You want to keep things spicy as much as possible over the years.

Money/Finances. If you haven't met Mr. Right, you really don't know how he will be in this department, but consider how you want him to be in your ideal dreams. Does he take care of the finances, or do you? Imagine how he would be and don't settle for anything less.

Work/Career. You want to find a man who loves what he does. If he's happy with his work/career, then he'll be happy in general and it will be one less thing to worry about. You want to find a man with a good job or a career that he loves and is good at. There is nothing more attractive than a man who is skilled at what he does and who thrives in his work place.

Social Life. One partner is usually more social than the other. Hopefully you find someone who is at least somewhat close to you in this department. It can be frustrating if you love to socialize and your partner is a recluse. Observe this in the men you date but as you sketch out your Relationship Map think about the kind of social life you would like to have.

Meals. This may seem like a silly thing to consider but since you're creating your dream relationship on paper you may as well write it out all down, even down to the detail of meals. We spend a lot of our waking hours eating and so it's

Chapter 9 What You Need to Know About Him Before Getting Physical

an important part of our lives. Do you see yourself cooking dinner every night, or would you love to find a guy who loves to cook? Do you love to dine out most nights? Is it important to you that you find a vegan partner? Write it all down but be open to all possibilities.

Travel/Vacations. Would you love to travel the world? If so, you will want to find someone who wants to do the same. Write down all the places you want to go. Or maybe you're a homebody and have no real desire to travel much. That's okay, write it down and look for a guy who agrees!

Long Distance Relationships. Before we got married, my husband and I had a long distance relationship for some time. It definitely has its advantages, as it kept the relationship fresh. We missed each other terribly and couldn't wait to see each other. When we did see each other it was passionate and exciting. We knew we were totally committed to each other, and we spoke several times a day on the phone.

I think the key factor here is that you are open and honest about the parameters of the relationship. Are you going to be completely exclusive? If not, what is okay and what isn't? Discuss how long you see this going on, and how you're going to spend time together. You need to get together occasionally, and in the meantime you can do Skype, email, text, call, send packages to each other, and so on.

You have to trust each other, so don't grill the other person or act jealous if you can't get a hold of them for some reason. You have to be secure in the relationship and in yourself to make it work. And hopefully it is only temporary.

FINDING MR. RIGHT

This is the most difficult part of the process, and I wish I could give you clear-cut answers here. I realize it isn't easy to meet men, especially men you would consider marrying. I do know that there are good men out there, and there are plenty of men who are looking for someone like you. Although I can't tell you *where* or *when* you will meet him, I can tell you that everything in this book will prepare you for when you do. All you need to do is follow everything to the letter, and you will draw more men to you and you will find that men are more attracted to you than ever before. You will definitely have more confidence because you will be fully prepared and know what to do when you do meet a great guy.

It's just a matter of time—most people get married, at least once in their lives—it will happen for you too. Just focus on preparing yourself right now so that you are completely ready for when it happens. Create your Man Plan, and your Relationship Map. Work on your Sexual History Chart and clear out any cob-webs in your mind/heart that might be holding you back. Practice your Pre-sex Pow-Wow and make yourself as attractive as possible. Get out as often as you can and go to every event, party, gathering, and so on. Make yourself seen. And don't give up before the miracle happens!

Next we are going to go over some of the key principles in awakening feelings of love in the man of your choice. You possess more power in this process than you might imagine.

Chapter 10
The Art of Awakening Love

The premise of this book is that by not getting sexually involved too soon (before love happens and a commitment is made), you will have a greater chance of developing a healthy relationship that is based on love, trust, and respect. Once this is accepted you need to know *how* to build love, trust, and respect.

The first thing to know is that you do possess the power to awaken love in the man of your choice. You do not have to hope or wish for it to just "click" with someone. The power is within *you*. This doesn't mean that men don't play a role or share some of the responsibility—but the message in these pages should inspire you to realize your full potential as a woman.

Obviously, there is natural chemistry between people and not everyone will be attracted to you. There are also many outside factors that could play a role in the development, or the demise, of a potential relationship—such as timing (he just got a great job offer overseas), geographical issues (he lives in another city), people who surround the two of you (his mother or sisters whispering in his ear, for example), health issues (one of you just came down with an illness), or any number of other situations that you cannot control. But, if you follow the guidelines in this book, when you meet a great guy who seems to have great potential, you will have the tools necessary to trigger powerful feelings within him. He will be charmed, smitten, fascinated, intrigued, and eventually he will fall deeply in love. But remember, it is a process and it requires great patience and self-control.

Many women throughout the world are loved and adored by their husbands and boyfriends. Some of them may have never read a book on the subject, but instinctively they know what attracts men, and they have the ability to create harmonious, loving relationships. Or possibly their mothers, sisters, or friends offered various methods that work.

Then there are women who are *not* adored and loved—their mates may care very much for them and even be completely devoted to them. But they don't *cherish* them. All of these women may be equally attractive or intelligent. They all have their strengths and weaknesses. So what is the difference? The difference is that women either consciously or unconsciously apply the principles involved in awakening true love, or they apply some of them and end up with a watered down version (consciously or not).

Some women naturally possess the qualities described in Chapter 12: *The Ten Qualities Men Find Most Irresistible in a Lifetime Mate* and they seem intuitively to understand men. They have a way about them that draws out the best in a man. Men find them adorable, delightful, and fascinating. Some women can articulate what is going on and what it is about them that makes them successful with men, and others are oblivious. The smartest thing a woman can do for herself is study the underlying principles that create and awaken true love so that she can approach a relationship with confidence and purpose, rather than simply hoping things will work out.

Chapter 10 The Art of Awakening Love

This chapter outlines the art of awakening love, which is broken down into two sections: 1) Who You Are, and 2) What you Do. But first, let's talk about how to determine if he's in love...

How to Tell if He's in Love With You

When a man is in love, he can't seem to get you out of his mind. As hard as he tries, he cannot live without you. He finds himself doing more for you and with you than anyone else. He is compelled to be with you, to give to you, to call you, to think of you, and to protect you. He has an overwhelming desire to make you happy. He is also sexually drawn to you and wants to be affectionate with you.

The more in love a man is, the more he will give. He will give more of his time, attention, and money. The look in his eyes will also give it away. In the movie *Shadowlands,* the character played by Debra Winger says to Anthony Hopkins, "Now you look at me properly," when it became obvious that he was deeply in love with her. You could just see the love welling up in his eyes.

He will also begin to take the relationship more seriously. He won't want to keep the relationship a secret, he will want to shout it from the rooftops. Once you experience this kind of love, you will never want to settle for anything less. I'm fortunate to say that I have this kind of love with my husband, Michael. Marrying him was the best decision I ever made. I followed everything in this book, to the letter, and it worked. I feel adored, cherished, pampered, and loved. I know that he cares about my welfare and he accepts me as I am. To begin with, Michael is just naturally a good man, and he had a great childhood full of love and stability, as well as a great example of a loving marriage with his parents, who are still happily married after 59 years. But I worked hard to do everything right. I kept sex at bay for a very long time and made sure we had a solid foundation of love, trust, commitment, and so on. I knew he loved me long before we made love, and so finally consummating the relationship simply added a new level of intimacy that strengthened the relationship. Was he always happy with the arrangement? No! He tried to change my mind about having sex more times than I'd like to admit. At times he begged, pleaded, whined, pouted, and cajoled. But he never left me. He never threatened to break up with me because of not having sex early on in the relationship. He was just frustrated and sexually attracted to me. He's a very sexual person so it was difficult! But he loved me. He wanted me. Sex wasn't the primary reason he was with me. We loved each other's company and we talked on the phone for hours, as well as spent lots of time together. I got to know Michael really well—long enough for me to feel completely safe. He made me feel safe because his feelings for me never wavered; they only deepened. He proved himself to be responsible, trustworthy, honest, compassionate, and understanding. He always did what he said he was going to do. And despite our arguments about not having sex, we generally got along really well and adored each other. I feel so fortunate to finally have met the love of my life. It took a long time and it was a rough road, but my dreams finally came true. I was finally *true to myself*, and then everything fell into place.

WHAT MEN FALL IN LOVE WITH

If you ask men, they have no real idea why or how they fall in love, they only know they feel incredible when they are with the woman they love. And while men don't *need* to know how the falling in love process works, women do.

Some people are just not meant to be together and no matter what, love is not going to grow. In most cases, however, there is much within your control. To simplify the process, it could be said that men fall in love with two things: *who you are* and *what you do*.

Who You Are

In chapter 12 we discuss the qualities men find most irresistible in a lifetime mate. If you strive to develop those traits and become an adorable, fresh, radiant woman, men will be drawn to you. Think in terms of *inner* and *outer* qualities. Inner qualities include calmness, peacefulness, happiness, understanding, high self-esteem, and having strong character.

The outer qualities refer to your appearance, which should be feminine, soft, neat, clean, and not overly sexy. Men love a radiant, healthy glow, sparkling eyes, and clear skin. And you always want to wear a big smile. Other outer qualities are being spunky, outspoken, playful, and charming.

All of these qualities will attract men to you, enhance your relationships, and bring you more joy. But being a great woman is often not enough. There are plenty of great women who don't have men knocking down their doors to get at them. Who you are is important, but equally important is *what you do*.

What You Do

Most relationships don't last, and even the ones that do, aren't always happy. Love will not always just happen naturally. You may do things that completely prevent love from fully developing. You may be beautiful, charming, intelligent, and witty. But if you don't know how to treat a man, you probably won't be able to hold on to him for long. You certainly won't have the kind of love described earlier in this chapter, and in chapter 1.

As you treat a man with respect, appreciate all that he does for you, admire his strengths, and learn to trust him, he naturally falls in love with you (as long as you are also a challenge to get, and follow all of the other steps).

Why he Might Not Be Falling in Love

Relationships can be very complex. There isn't always a simple answer. But in most cases, these are the reasons why he is not falling in love.

1)   **You had sex too soon.** This is the number one reason why he isn't falling in love with you. How can he? It's all over—the chase, the drama, the excitement of getting to know you and winning you over. You have already let him in to your inner sanctum and there's nowhere to go from there. I know it's painful to admit and to acknowledge the reality of this, but it's true. Do your Sexual History Chart and, if you're brutally honest, you'll see.

2)   **You don't have chemistry.** Sometimes a relationship is just not meant to be. Everything may be clicking for you, but he is not feeling the same way. It happens and it's especially frustrating if you really like him. But if this happens to you, just move on. There is very little, if anything, that you can do in this situation. You don't want to make a fool out of yourself by trying to get this guy to like you, and if the chemistry just isn't there, it probably never will be.

Chapter 10 The Art of Awakening Love

3) ***You chased him too much.*** Remember, men are the natural pursuers. It ruins the flow of things when you turn the tables and begin doing their job. It scares them off, pure and simple. The relationship is not necessarily ruined if you made the mistake of chasing him—simply stop doing it and see if he comes after you. If he doesn't, move on. If he does, you reined it in before you turned him off. And I'm not saying that making the first moves (like asking him out) *never* works—there are plenty of stories out there of women pursuing the men and they are happy couples to this day. But in general it just works better to let him chase you. *Note:* If a man says something like, "Here's my card, why don't you give me a call sometime?" I suggest you respond with, "I'd prefer you to call me." Don't be afraid to gently put the responsibility back on him, even though he may seem put-off at first.

Most men like women who insist that they do the pursuing. We all know that men are competitive by nature and love a challenge. Imagine you have several men who are top chess players. They are entering a world-class competition. Each of them wants to win more than anything. But what if one of them learned some secret formula that gave him the ability to win every game, no matter what? Imagine what that would be like for this man. Eventually, winning would not be so exciting anymore and he would lose interest. Because *winning* isn't really what it is about—it's about the *challenge* and *excitement* of the journey. Apply this same concept to men you are dating. There has to be that element of *not knowing if he can win* that must be present in order for him to feel really good about winning *you*. He has to feel that he earned it. During the match (or any sport/game, or dating) neither opponent knows how the game is ultimately going to

Love Before Sex

turn out, but they are making their moves and doing their best. If it's an easy game that is over in three minutes, trust me, it is not as exciting (for anyone) than if it goes into overtime and keeps everyone on their toes, wondering how it's going to end up. The athlete that had to practice, train and work extra hard to win feels the proudest of their accomplishment and it means all that much more to them.

4) **You lack certain qualities that men find desirable in women.** Erika, 39, gets plenty of sexual attention from men, but no one wants a serious relationship with her. She is loud, at times obnoxious, pushy, and very opinionated. She also dresses provocatively and has an extremely sexy look. Yet, she can't understand why men don't want her for anything but sex. The saddest part is that Erika isn't willing to look at herself and admit and that changes need to be made. If you're having trouble attracting men in general, study the traits in chapter 12 and determine the areas you need to work on. Obviously, there is someone for everyone and you don't have to be all of the things I list—but haven't you noticed that men, in general, are attracted to certain qualities, such as femininity, intelligence, happy, loving, strong yet vulnerable, outspoken but not pushy? You can also ask your close friends to give you feedback about your personality or character—ask them if they think any revamping is necessary. Do your research, gather information, and take inventory of yourself.

5) **You don't make him feel great when he's with you.** In the next section, we are going to cover the nine basic needs of a man. If these needs aren't met fairly consistently, he may not be able to fall deeply in love. He may like you a lot or grow to care for you, but he won't feel love in the deepest sense. A

man needs to feel respected, appreciated, admired, and understood. If he doesn't, he may not be inspired to make you his lifetime partner. If you find yourself criticizing him, however subtly, or you like to argue, control, or attempt to change him, you need to study the next section carefully and try making changes in the way you treat all men; especially the man you are seeing romantically.

6) ***He is incapable of loving anyone.*** Some men, no matter who you are or what you do, are simply unable to open up and actually love someone. Perhaps they suffered from severe childhood trauma, or they just didn't learn how to love. Although people can change and overcome these difficulties, the last thing you want to do is spend a lifetime trying to get someone to love you who just isn't capable. Moving on is the best choice.

7) ***It has nothing to do with you.*** Bad timing could be why some men won't allow themselves to fall in love. They just refuse to open up to the possibilities because of something else going on in their lives. Maybe he's seeing another woman or still trying to get over a past relationship. There could be any number of reasons. But don't use this as a cop-out, or an excuse to blame it on the guy. The fact is, if he's crazy about you he will overcome whatever obstacles stand in his way.

HOW TO MAKE HIM FEEL LIKE A MILLION BUCKS

Men fall in love with you as you supply them with what their souls cry out for. As you admire him for his strengths, appreciate all he does, show him understanding, and give him respect, a man becomes completely devoted to you. It's difficult to give a man these things consistently, but the more consistently you fulfill his needs, the more consistently you will feel cherished. Just be careful that you don't overdo this too early in the relationship when you're supposed to be a challenge—you don't want to seem like you are too in to him or too eager to please or be overly sacrificial. This is behavior to deepen his feelings over time and to develop a solid foundation for a long-term relationship. He also has to be worthy of this treatment, so you dole this treatment out over time, as you get to know and respect him.

Unfortunately, many women today are more concerned with what they're *getting* out of the relationship rather than having confidence that their needs will be met beyond all expectations when they give men what they need. You want men to give first, then you give back and always a little less.

HIS NINE BASIC NEEDS

1) **RESPECT**. A man must feel respected, especially by the woman he loves. Women want to be respected also, but in a different way and to a different degree. For a man to thrive and be happy, he must have the respect of the woman in his life. When a woman doesn't really respect a man, she often begins to destroy him. This may be quite obvious or very subtle. It usually begins with little criticisms. She may get irritated with the way he does things or his views on a situation. She doesn't fully trust him, or respect his judgment or leadership abilities. Many extremely successful men credit their success to the women in their lives. Truly amazing things can happen when a man is inspired by a wise, good woman.

How to Show Respect. I was having dinner with some friends of mine. I'll call them Cheri and William. They had been married for about a year at the time and I had never

Chapter 10 The Art of Awakening Love

seen them argue. I could see why. They were trying to decide on a particular investment. William thought it was an excellent opportunity, while Cheri felt it was too risky. The way Cheri chose to handle the situation was perfect. She didn't criticize him or his idealistic views. She didn't roll her eyes or make fun of him. She didn't argue his points. She simply said, "I feel nervous about the risk involved, but I trust your judgment. You know more about these particular investments than I do, and I'm sure you will do the right thing." This attitude made William feel respected and loved, and he was spared from being embarrassed in front of an outside person. Cheri called me a few weeks later to tell me that William chose not to invest because, as she said, "He didn't want to do something that would make me feel uneasy."

As this example illustrates, the main principle behind showing him respect is *trusting his judgment.* If you are with a man whose judgment you cannot trust, you need to reconsider your choice of men. You also never want to argue on and on with a man. It's okay to disagree and debate, but it's better to agree to disagree, while still letting him know that you respect him.

2) **ADMIRATION.** Just as you need to be cherished, men need to be admired. This is obvious and yet so few women ever really practice this. Some women are afraid that the man will expect that kind of treatment all the time, or they're afraid they're not up for the task. Then there's the problem of feeling phony or silly. But as you practice looking for things to admire in men, you see the pleasure it gives them. Admiration brings so much joy to the relationship. The added work is such a small investment considering the great

return. Men crave admiration. They long for it. They need it. And the woman who gives it to them is the one they will adore forever. It is rare for a man, especially these days, to find a woman who will show him admiration. And when he does find a woman who recognizes his strengths and actually comments on them, it's as though he's found a hidden treasure. He will long to be with her more and more. She becomes central to his happiness.

Many women today are too busy trying to get respect and admiration for *themselves*. They have their own accomplishments for which to seek attention. They figure, "Why should *I* work so hard to make *him* feel good? What about *me*?" Women who feel this way have never experienced the rewards of giving men the admiration they need. They see it as more work than it's worth, rather than a simple, easy thing to do for the return of tender love and a positive relationship. The more admiration you give, the more your love and appreciation for each other will grow. And if your admiration for him is sincere he will want to be with you simply because of the way he feels when he's with you.

How to Show Admiration

Find masculine traits to admire in your man. Look for things that have meaning for him. Men are not all that moved if you admire the way they dress, for example, or how prompt they are. As corny as it sounds, men do like to hear about how strong, smart, industrious, ingenious, and thoughtful they are. It may be awkward at first to point out these things, but wait for when the time is right and with a little practice it will become second nature. I always tell my husband how brilliant he is, and how I love his big, strong muscles—he loves it! He is also very good at fixing anything around the house, and so whenever he does I admire how creative he is and how he is so competent. It makes him feel appreciated but also admired for being a capable man who takes care of me. It makes him feel good so I try to not miss the opportunities. Here are some specific areas on which you can focus:

His Work

If you encourage him to talk to about his work, you'll find an entire treasure chest of things to admire. Most men take their work very seriously. A man appreciates a woman who is interested in what he does and who finds importance in his work. Men usually carry a lot of burdens and stress in this area of their lives—they need a good woman who is willing to listen and sympathize (women need this too, so hopefully you find a man who can reciprocate). You can say things like, ""You really have a lot of responsibility with your job. I'll bet you're very good at what you do." Or "How did you get to be so successful? You're so talented." Obviously, you want to be sincere and only say these things if they're true. The point is to find something about what they do and show admiration, on a consistent basis.

His Athleticism

Maybe he is gifted in athletics. Men love it when women notice their strengths in this area. You could say things like, "You're so athletic! I love to watch you in action!" or, "You're the best player out there. You're really strong!"

His Physique

Admiring a man's body makes a man feel great. Let him know his masculinity brings out the woman in you. I realize some of this might seem silly or embarrassing, but as you practice expressing yourself in this way, it will become more natural. And men will love it. They don't care how corny it is, as long as you mean what you say. They may laugh or tease you at first, but they won't want you to stop! Go ahead and say things like, "You're so big and strong, I just love your body!" and "I love having your big, strong arms around me. You make me feel so safe." Obviously, this kind of talk comes a little bit later in the relationship—if you do it too soon you could scare him away.

His Mental Abilities

Men also love it when their intellect is admired. Look for moments when his problem-solving skills come into play, such as his ability to negotiate a deal or the like. You could say things like, "I just love the fact that you are so smart. You are a walking encyclopedia! Or, "What would I do without you? You are really brilliant!" or, "I'm so glad you know so much. It makes me feel more secure."

His Overall Masculine Nature

There doesn't have to be a reason or specific occurrence for you to express your appreciation for his masculinity. You can simply give him a big hug and tell him you love how much of a *man* he is! The more you admire the *masculinity* in a man, the more *femininity* he will see in you. This will create a powerful chemistry between you and your mate. I have actually said all of these things to my husband, in some form or another over the years, and I can vouch that it brings out the best in a man!

3) **ACCEPTANCE.** Accepting a man means you accept *everything* about him. Bad habits, little quirks in his personality, the decisions he makes, what he does for a living, how he spends his time, how he deals with his problems, and so on. You may not like every aspect of the man, but if you're not accepting him as he is, then you are probably attempting to control him by nagging, complaining, criticizing, and the like. These things never work with men—they only succeed in driving them away eventually, or destroying the tender love you have worked so hard to create in the beginning of a relationship. And even if you do succeed in getting him to change his behavior for a time—typically, men end up being who they were to begin with, and they resort back to whatever behavior they exhibited before. The only difference is there is now a wall between you because he knows you don't approve of him on some level. Criticizing your man will only alienate him and destroy love. You want him to cherish and adore you, so you want to be cherish-able and adorable! So, you either want to end the relationship if you can't be comfortable with him exactly as he is, or you want to accept him as he is, flaws and all. And you hope that he will do the same for you! If you find yourself being critical, try to focus on whatever qualities in *yourself* that you need to work on. No doubt there's plenty to keep you busy because none of us are perfect.

4) **APPRECIATION.** If you want a man to cherish you, show him a lot of appreciation. Let him know through your words and actions that you appreciate who he is and all that he does for you. Appreciation and admiration go hand in hand. Giving him the impression that you like him just the way he is and that he is your hero makes him feel very appreciated, which in turn will make you feel very loved. Men often say, "She just seemed to *expect* it." A man wants to give of himself to a woman, but he has a serious problem if she just expects this treatment and isn't really appreciative. Think about the times you have given someone a gift or have done something special for them. If they thanked you, praised you, and/or loved it, then you received more pleasure, right? I know a man who was constantly buying his girlfriend gifts for no particular reason. I asked him what it was that compelled him to do this. He said, "Whenever I give my girlfriend anything, whether it's expensive or not, she just loves it and appreciates it so much. I just can't wait to do it again and again. It makes me feel great!"

How to Show Appreciation.

Look for opportunities to say how glad you are that he is a part of your life. Don't allow moments to slip by where you can show gratitude and give praise when he does something for you. Then you can *show* him how much you appreciate him by doing nice things for *him*. There are many ways you can give back. Men love it when you cook for them. Small gifts are okay at times, but most men prefer you do something nice for them. You could also say something like, "You are so good to me. How did I get to be so lucky?" or, "You really are my knight in shining armor!" Thank you for being so generous." Even if you don't like the particular present he gave you, he will appreciate your thanking him for the gesture and it's always best to focus on the fact that he went out of his way to get you something he thought you would like.

5) **COOPERATION.** A man appreciates a woman who is flexible and cooperates with him. Unfortunately, being cooperative isn't always so easy to do, especially when you think your way is better. That's another reason why it's so important to find someone with whom you are highly compatible—it's easier to avoid power struggles. The sad part is that most of the situations in which you become stubborn or difficult are usually unimportant in the big scheme of things.

Men need cooperation for many reasons. I'm not suggesting that you subordinate yourself to men simply for the sake of keeping the peace. Of course you should speak your mind when you feel it's necessary, maintain your own opinions, and be your own person. But if you want *harmony* in your relationship, and your goal is to obtain the highest level of love, then you'll want to find ways to show some level of cooperation and flexibility in dealing with men. Men don't want a woman who fights them at every turn. I often observe that when women are with men they don't want to cooperate with, it is because they were with the wrong men. It's often a compatibility issue. Either you don't respect that man's views or you didn't like the way he approached life in general. If you're unhappy in the relationship it's going to come out in the form of not being cooperative.

I believe it is more effective to show disappointment and hurt rather than to yell, berate, or argue. It's okay to be angry and to express that anger, but screaming, being irate, and showing hostility are never effective. How often have you been totally justified in being angry with a man only to alienate him? When you express hurt or disappointment, a man is more likely to apologize. There is a proverb that says, "By fighting you never get enough, but by yielding you get more than you expected."

How to be Cooperative.

You need to ask yourself if what you are fighting for is really worth it. If you did it his way, then would you be violating your own moral code? If not, then why not try to be flexible and see what happens? You may want to save your energy for when you do feel strongly about having your own way. Even if you disagree, you can choose to support him in his decision. You do this not to acquiesce, but to show your love, understanding, and trust in your man. Your relationship shouldn't be a competition where you each fight for equal rights. You want to do your part no matter what the other person is doing, simply because you love them and want to create a beautiful relationship that is healthy and harmonious. You could always use this line, "I would prefer to do it this way, but if you feel strongly about it, I will support you in your decision."

6) **TRUST.** It's difficult to surrender to anything or anyone. And you do want to take your time and discover if you truly can trust the man you're seeing. Although I like to think it's rare, there are men who just want to use you and get whatever it is they want from you. But once you've met your dream man and you have gotten to know enough about him to begin to let go and open up your heart, do so wholeheartedly. One woman I know, Nina, 58, had never trusted men in general. But once she did, she noticed a huge difference. "I was so tired of nit-picking about meaningless things with Andrew. I had been saying I was going to leave him for two years, yet I stayed. So I decided to stop saying I was leaving, and just surrender to the relationship. The

minute I did that, Andrew began talking marriage. There was such a huge difference in the way he treated me. He told me he loved me more often. He would call me during the day just to see how I was doing. He was much more loving. I guess he couldn't fully love me before because he sensed my lack of commitment. He saw that I always had one foot out the door. Once he saw that I had really surrendered to the relationship, the floodgates opened, and it has been wonderful."

You obviously don't want to totally surrender who you are, and you don't want to surrender too soon. But you do want to let go and trust your man slowly throughout the relationship, and at deeper levels, the longer you are together. When you show a man that you trust him, it causes him to want to rise to the occasion and not let you down.

How to Show Trust

The best way to show trust is to sit back and allow him to lead. It's always within his nature to do so; therefore, it requires very little on your part. Let him take care of things for a change. You can initially do this as an experiment, simply to see what happens and how he responds to your new attitude. You don't need to tell him what you're doing. You can give him the freedom to make most of the decisions and do things his way as much as possible. If you don't like the choices he makes and the way he does things, then there is a chance you're with the wrong person. Or, you may need to say something like, "I'm just not comfortable doing that. Could you come up with another idea?"

I know this sounds old-fashioned, but I see a lot of women making the mistake of trying to control everything and taking over. Men may go along with it because it's easier than fighting, but they don't always like it. They would love for you to trust them and their judgment sometimes. Back off and try showing some trust in him. Once you do he will have the space to take action. If you don't, he could feel inadequate and not needed. Men sometimes end up becoming more passive until women think they're lazy. Soon the women think that the men always leave everything to them, which just isn't the case. I know a woman who has had a few bad experiences with men. She now appears to be paranoid. She's afraid he won't call when he says he will. She feels she has to get him to verbally commit to when they will see each other again. This, of course, kills feelings of trust and puts a real strain on him and on the relationship.

7) **FREEDOM**. We all want to feel as though we are able to be who we want to be, do what we want to do, and believe what we want to believe. Men can't stand to feel confined, tied down, or pressured. It's more the *feeling* of freedom that they love more than anything else.

You never want to act like you own the man you are with. A man will devote himself to you, but he doesn't want you to make him feel imprisoned. Never boss him around or constantly tell him how things should be done. Trust that he can figure it out and that he will do a great job. Even if he doesn't, it's better to let him know you do believe in him versus trying to control him and to show doubt. Men get turned off by women bossing them around all the time and they often will do the opposite of what you want, just to prove that they can't be controlled.

Other ways women try to control men: by making suggestions, hints, or outright demands. Some women try to manipulate men into doing it their way and basically attempt to run their lives. Very few men like being controlled. Many, if not most, men will not put with it from the outset. Others may seemingly accept it for awhile, but all men eventually will begin to resent the woman who tries to control them. Instead of love growing and deepening over time, it begins to be destroyed, little by little.

For the sake of the relationship, don't try to control him. Instead, try accepting him as he is and allow him the freedom to be his own man. He will adore you when you do.

How to give him his freedom.

Here's a checklist of ways to give a man freedom:

- Don't quiz him, nag him, try to get him to call, or see you according to your timetable and desires. Let him decide for himself when he wants to be with you.
- Don't tell him how he should be spending his time and don't make plans for him without consulting with him first.
- Don't hint about a future together unless you are engaged. This can make him feel trapped by someone who wants to take him over.
- Don't worry about him when he is not with you. Keep in mind that he is a big boy and can take care of himself. Men don't want to marry their mothers—healthy ones, that is!

8) **UNDERSTANDING.** Travis, 54, a real estate developer, had just purchased his first big deal—a piece of property in a prime location where he could build a shopping center. He had worked hard for years for this opportunity. He had to put as much energy as possible into the project. Jaleen, his girlfriend, didn't seem to understand the importance of Travis's work. She constantly tried to distract him. She would call his office incessantly, insisting that he spend more time with her. If he were late due to extended meetings, then he knew he'd be in big trouble.

Travis really cared about Jaleen and wanted to be with her, but sometimes he just couldn't break away from his project. He had a lot of responsibility, and he wished she was more supportive. He tried to explain his position, but Jaleen couldn't shake the feeling of being neglected. She couldn't see the situation from his perspective, she only saw her own. They fought a lot about the issue until Travis finally began pulling away. The relationship with Jaleen brought more aggravation than he could tolerate in his life.

The pressures and responsibilities can be enormous, not to mention the unexpected problems that arise. A man desperately needs a mate who is very understanding and supportive in this area.

When he calls and says he will be late or even cancels a date with you, imagine the difference in how he will feel about you when you say something, "It's okay, I understand. You take care of the problems at work, I'll talk to you tomorrow." Versus, "I can't believe you are doing this to me again! How can you cancel on me at the last minute? What am I supposed to do now?" As he works into the night and then drives home, which response will have him tenderly thinking about you, wanting to see you? An understanding attitude causes a man to want to see you as soon as possible, simply to be with the good woman he loves.

Note: I'm a real stickler for being on time, returning calls/texts/emails promptly, keeping commitments, and the like. I'm not talking about accepting a man who is flaky all the time, or who cancels frequently. You'll know the difference—follow your intuition and you'll know when to be understanding versus when to express your displeasure with his behavior.

9) **ENCOURAGEMENT.** By encouraging a man, you give him the clear message that you believe in him and that you are behind him, no matter what. You are the positive force in his life when he feels down. The more you give a man encouragement, the more he will turn to you. You want your mate to come to you with his goals, his triumphs, his defeats. This is what builds a bond between two people and adds depth to a relationship.

Encouragement is important in making a man feel as though you are truly on his side and behind him every step of the way. He needs to know that you believe in him and that you have faith in his abilities. He will begin to feel that you are the one woman who really knows how to build him up and encourage him.

How to Show Encouragement

When a man expresses fears, doubts, worries, or disappointments, you can then encourage him by saying something like, "I know you are going to do great. You are so smart and capable. I know you will do the right thing. I believe in you."

You don't want to give him advice or try to solve his problems. You do want to focus on encouraging him as a way to help instill confidence. He will figure out his own solutions. Right now he just needs an encouraging friend who believes in him. He will open up as he feels safe to do so. The last thing you want to do, if he opens up to you, is say something like, "I told you so!" or "Why did you do that?!" Instead, let him know by your words and mannerisms that you care, sympathize, and understand.

Don't Give Too Much!

Even though I believe you should give men what they need, you don't want to give too much. If you focus only on pleasing him, serving him, and making him happy, he will get spoiled, and this can bring out bad behavior. He will begin to take advantage of you, his feelings for you could begin to cool, and of course, you'll end up feeling used. Your inner voice and intuition will let you know when to pull back and give less.

HOW TO DEAL WITH HIM WHEN HE SEEMS DISTANT OR COLD.

If a man seems aloof, you may have given too much. You may have tried to control him, or not shown your appreciation for what he has done for you. Or, it could have nothing to do with you. In any case, you probably need to back off and give him some space. Focus on your own life and interests and let him make his way back to you. Don't constantly ask what's wrong. You could ask once, but if he doesn't confide in you then let it go and just try to follow all of the other suggestions in this book.

I promise you that if you strive to be the kind of woman that a man would want to take home to meet the family; the kind of woman he'd want to be the mother to his children; the kind of woman who understands men and what they need; a woman who cares about herself and doesn't just give of herself to someone who doesn't love her—I can almost guarantee you that he will fall madly in love and feel like the luckiest man alive. You don't have to be perfect, or be all of these things all the time. But in general if you're striving to be this kind of woman, men will notice and you will stand out as special. Study these points and try to make them a part of you. If you need a little more help with rebuilding your self-esteem, the next chapter will be helpful...

Chapter 11
Increase Self-Esteem

Maybe you already enjoy a high level of self-esteem. You may be a confident woman who feels worthy of love and in your ability to attract men. If so, this chapter may be a refresher course for you. But maybe your self-esteem has been bruised as a result of childhood trauma, and/or years of dysfunctional relationships. Perhaps you are disillusioned and frustrated by getting sucked into relationships that seem great in the beginning, only to dissolve down the road. It could be that you have been deceived and used sexually by one or more men, or you lacked the ability to see the red flags soon enough.

Some women engage in regular "booty calls" or go to clubs and take home a new guy every weekend. It's possible that they truly enjoy the experiences they have, and it isn't my intention to make any kind of moral judgments about these things. I have no problem with casual sex if that's what you want and you can truly handle it. The problem is many women are not fully *conscious* about their choices. If low self-esteem and lack of confidence is what's driving the casual sex, then it isn't healthy. For example, if your self-esteem is at an all-time low, you may say yes to sex because you feel that sex and your body are all you have to offer. You may be desperately hoping that the guy will develop feelings for you but you lead with your sexuality out of fear of him losing interest. You may not be conscious that this is what's happening, but if you take an honest look at yourself and your sexual behavior, you may discover that you were having sex with men you didn't know and love for all the wrong reasons. And honestly, is there a good reason to share so much of yourself with someone who doesn't really care about you?

The other problem with "unconscious" casual sex is that it doesn't get you what you want. If only casual sex truly is all you want, then that's what you'll get. But if what you want is love, commitment, and the possibility of a real future with someone, then casual sex can be more self-destructive than facilitative.

It is not within the scope of this book to go into great detail about this topic, but in this chapter I share several important points about building self-esteem, such as the Ten Steps to Higher Self-Esteem. I also think it's important to reflect on your past relationships, honestly asking yourself *why* you had sex when you did with each partner, by creating a *Sexual History Chart*.

Defining High Self-Esteem

A person with high self-esteem feels worthy of love and commands respect simply because of how she feels about herself. She feels in control of her life and her relationships. No one is able to take advantage of her because she knows how to set limits and boundaries. She is in touch with her feelings. She knows when something doesn't feel right and she does something about it. She quickly takes action in order to make the situation more appropriate. She stands up for herself when necessary. She makes sure her needs are met. She knows who she is and what she wants in life. She knows what her values are. She accepts herself as a woman who is growing. She strives to improve what she can, and she accepts that which she is unable to change. She is at peace with herself. She doesn't blame others for her problems. She knows that she is in control of her destiny.

A woman with high self-esteem is also willing to take more risks. She is able to walk away from a bad relationship even though she knows it will be painful. She is able to venture out on her own if that's the best thing for her to do. She looks for opportunities to improve herself and to live up to her full potential.

When you have high self-esteem, you become more interesting and desirable to others, especially men. You stand a little taller and smile a little brighter. You feel more whole and that's how you appear. Your body movements are more natural. You appear relaxed and calm.

We all want to be around people who are confident and who seem at ease in almost every situation. We are drawn to those who are healthy and radiant. And we are turned off by those who are needy, depressed, and empty.

What High Self-Esteem Offers

- You enjoy more peace of mind.
- You exude confidence and self-assurance.
- You make healthier decisions.
- You attract better partners.
- You choose better partners.
- You have the courage to say no to things that are harmful to you (such as casual sex!).
- You are able to say yes to the things that are good for you.

- You don't worry as much about what others think about you.
- You don't second-guess yourself as much.
- You are able to walk away from hurtful situations and people.
- You have a more positive and grateful attitude.
- You feel hopeful about your future and feel worthy of love, kindness, and being pampered.

A Look at Low Self-Esteem

People with low self-esteem tend to be pessimistic and negative. They see the glass as half-empty. They often feel awkward, shy, and uncomfortable in social settings. They often take comments the wrong way and feel slighted a lot by others. Studies show that people with low self-esteem tend to also suffer from depression and exhibit a lot of anger. A person with low self-esteem is needy and unable to say no when she doesn't feel comfortable in a situation. As it relates to sex, she may have sex with men she's not in love with and possibly doesn't even like. She operates from fear—fear of losing him, fear of not being loved, fear of not being accepted, fear of abandonment. A person with low self-esteem subconsciously says, "I can't imagine being in a relationship where he completely adores me and tells me often how much he loves me. I've never had that and probably never will."

A person with low self-esteem is unable to be honest with herself. She has a difficult time seeing her relationships with others as they really are and instead finds ways of justifying her involvements. A person with low self-esteem blames others for her problems rather than taking responsibility.

If this describes you, I would suggest you do some self-examination and work on yourself... see a good therapist or someone who can help you regain your sense of confidence and self-love. It's very difficult to follow the suggestions in this book if you're struggling with low self-esteem. But there are answers and help is readily available. For a start, try implementing the 10 Steps to Higher Self-Esteem.

10 STEPS TO HIGHER SELF-ESTEEM
STEP 1: BE HONEST WITH YOURSELF

If you're unable or unwilling to be honest with yourself about who you are and what is going on in your life, then it's impossible to learn to accept yourself and develop high self-esteem. An important area to focus on is your feelings. When you're in pain, acknowledge that you are in pain. If you are experiencing emotional pain because you had sex with someone and now he's not calling, then acknowledge that feeling and the cause. Many women avoid the truth and blame it on something else. They generalize and say things like "What a creep! Men are all dogs. He was obviously afraid of commitment. I'm better off without him." Maybe this man did mislead you, but that's not the point. The point is, in every situation, you need to be honest with yourself as to what you are really feeling, and why. A more honest comment might be, "I really wish I hadn't slept with him. I sort of lost my mind in the heat of the moment, and now I realize that it was just too soon. I'm feeling hurt right now because he's not calling." It's healthy to acknowledge your feelings no matter what they are—but then take responsibility. In the above scenario, her concern shouldn't be why he didn't call, but rather why she chose to sleep with him so soon. Being honest allows you to get to the heart of the problem.

When you acknowledge the truth, you can then learn from your mistakes and begin to make the necessary changes to get on the right track. You can come up with some new behaviors that work *for* you and not against you. But if you continue to blame the situation on others or justify your behavior, then you become stuck in the position of victim.

Changing negative patterns requires taking a good look at your past relationships and the most effective way of doing that is by putting it all down on paper, on what I call a *"Sexual History Chart"*. You can't know the solutions until you know what the problems are or have been. As difficult as this exercise is, it will be the best thing you ever did for yourself. What a revelation it is to see on paper the history of the past few years or even decades and analyzing it to the point of seeing clear patterns. You will be able to gain a better understanding of your relationships and your approach to the sexual aspect of those relationships. You will learn what your true motives were and what you were feeling. At one time you may have been in denial or were unaware of certain feelings you had, but after doing this exercise you will be able to see it all much more accurately.

SEXUAL HISTORY CHART

A Sexual History Chart is a powerful process whereby you write down the man's name that you had sex with, a brief summary of how you met and who made the first sexual advance, and how it happened. As a result of doing this exercise, you will be able to discern what really happened in your past relationships—for example, you may have become sexually involved with someone because you were afraid you would lose them, or because you drank too much and lost all self-control, or because you thought you had more of a connection than you really did.

Here is a sample chart:

Clarissa's Sexual History Chart

Nathan	Andrew	Alan	Patrick
19 years old. Met at a party. Had sex on first date. Had no discussion about this time. Did not rush into sex. Continued to date for about six months.	23 years old. Wanted to do it right this time. Did not rush into sex. Discussed commitment beforehand. He told me that he loved me. After one year we broke up because we fought too much and it wasn't leading to marriage.	25 years old. I was at a low in my life. Very depressed, unemployed. Just wanted someone around. He was there, we were friends at first, so we had that bond. I wouldn't sex with him for a long time. We did discuss being monogamous and we did express loving feelings for each other before having sex.	Present: 28 years old. Fell in love before we became sexual. We are already discussing marriage and the relationship is not based on sex.
I had sex with him essentially because I didn't know how to say no! I thought I had to, and I guess I wanted to feel wanted by someone. I really felt that I loved ihm, but now I know it wasn't true love at all.	I loved him but I still felt something was missing. Even though he said he loved me, he did not want to marry me and that hurt (even though I had my doubts about him). I didn't wait long enough because our commitment wasn't strong enough. Felt like I lost a part of myself.	Because we made a commitment before having sex, and because I knew I did not want to marry Alan, I didn't have those horrible feelings of being used. But I did have the emptiness because the relationship wasn't based on love and there was no future. Total lack of fulfillment and real sadness. Also, something wasn't right. I was in it for the wrong reasons.	Finally, I feel completely loved, adored, cherished. He truly respects me and my values. Feel extremely secure within the relationship. I know that his feelings are sincere and not about sex, even though he is a very sexual person. I have finally learned that building love has nothing to do with sex and I finally know what it's like to be cherished.

Love Before Sex

We can see how Clarissa's sexual behavior changed over the years. She made the decision to be sexual for many reasons. Once, she was very depressed, unemployed, down and out. Another time, she was lonely and in need of some companionship. Seeing these reasons can help her see the problems more clearly. She can see her part in the process. She can see that in order to avoid falling into sexual, dead-end relationships, she can improve her self-esteem and develop her own happiness and fulfillment. Also, her values changed over the years. As she experienced the pain of having sex too soon, she intuitively knew to try new behavior in the next relationship. As she finally made the decision to abstain until she was in a committed relationship, she was able to experience a deeper kind of love. She finally got what she had wanted all along but not just because she met the "right" guy. She achieved a deeper kind of love because of her own efforts to change.

The purpose of doing this exercise is not to beat yourself up or to elicit shame—it's meant to be *empowering*. We have all heard the phrase, *The Truth shall Set You Free*—when you become brutally honest with yourself as to where you have been, and where you are now, you are then free to determine where you want to go. You may have lived with blinders on for a time—maybe you didn't want to think too hard about what you were doing, or you didn't feel good about yourself. But now it's time to take full responsibility for yourself and face the Truth of your past choices and the things that happened to you. As painful and difficult as this might be right now, in the end it will set you free. You might want to do this exercise with the support of a professional—maybe a therapist or skilled Life/Relationship Coach, or a good friend who you can trust to keep your information private. Remember that you are doing this to learn about yourself so that you can make better choices in the future.

You may not need to write down every single sexual partner you have had, (particularly if the number is high)—you might want to write down only the most recent or most significant relationships. If you're older, you may wonder if this exercise is even necessary. Trust the process and just do it. I had many women in their 60s and even a few in their 70s attend my seminars, and many of them sadly claimed they had never had a man be truly in love with them. It is never too late to change and to have a second chance at life, and romance! But right now take a good, honest look at your most recent significant relationships and try to pinpoint what led up to becoming sexual...was there any discussion prior to becoming physical? Were any feelings exchanged? Go through all the questions and do some soul-searching. Self-honesty is the key to successfully completing the Sexual History Chart.

STEP 2: ELIMINATE THE NEGATIVES FROM YOUR LIFE

You can't grow if there is something in your life that stunts you. That something could be drugs, alcohol, a person, unhealthy eating patterns, an addictive relationship, a job that you hate, or anything else that is holding you back from achieving happiness. Growth then becomes a matter of letting go, eliminating, or leaving behind that which is holding you back. It's when you *resist* letting go that the real pain increases. When you hold on to something that is obviously causing you pain, your self-esteem inevitably suffers.

You need to decide what you will accept as part of your life and what you won't accept. When you say goodbye, once and for all, to unhealthy relationships or "situations", then the growth process can begin, and you also begin to draw to you a higher quality of men. But you need a clean slate in order to begin the journey.

Life is a process of letting go. We begin by letting go of the warmth and security of our mother's womb and making our way into the world. We let go of crawling, or our baby teeth, of the security of staying home when we reach kindergarten age. In adulthood we might have to let go of friends, family, a bad marriage, or jobs to pursue new opportunities. We have to see this letting go as positive. It may be difficult to let go, but ultimately, we make it harder on ourselves if we don't let go.

Think back on your life and bring to mind all of the things you have let go. Now think about how well you handled each situation. You obviously survived the ordeal. Of course, losing a friend or relative to death is more difficult than losing your favorite jacket. But even with death, we miraculously seem able to recover. It's when we are going through it that it seems so hard. Just remember: *This too shall pass.* Nothing will last forever.

Many of you reading this are in a relationship that you know you must let go of if you want to grow, and if you want to be available for the right guy. You're holding on partly because the pain you know you will experience frightens you more than the idea of staying. But I want to encourage you to reframe the situation. Instead of feeling down and negative about having to "give up something"—get excited about "being free" of whatever negativity that thing/person brings you. Get excited about being free to meet someone of real quality who can love and cherish you the way you want to be loved and cherished. Get excited about all of the possibilities that will open up to you the minute you free yourself from whatever it is that is holding you back. It's a time to celebrate, not mope!

STEP 3: PRACTICE SELF-ACCEPTANCE

Most of us find some aspect of ourselves to dislike. We think our noses are too big, or we're too short or too fat or not educated enough. Many people think they're not pretty enough, thin enough, or attractive enough in general. Very few people are completely satisfied with everything about themselves, and if they were, we might think they were arrogant. Even people with high self-esteem dislike certain things about themselves. Yet, people with high self-esteem do something about the traits they are able to change. And they accept the traits they can't change.

If you have suffered from low self-esteem, then you are familiar with feeling inadequate. I hope you'll take my word for it when I say that it really is all attitude. It's what you think about yourself, and you can "act as if" until you believe it yourself. Men are attracted to confidence, as are women. Carry yourself as if you're the queen of the land—hold your head high, give good eye contact, and speak up so people can hear you. Don't come off as arrogant, but do be sure of yourself.

One of the biggest mistakes women make is that they put themselves down in front of others. Don't do this, especially around men. There's no reason to be self-deprecating or apologetic. Women tend to do this a lot more than men do, but it isn't necessary. Also, try not to compare yourself to other women. You have your strengths, just as we all do, and there's no reason for you to hold yourself up to someone else. Believe in yourself and be your own best friend.

Accepting Being Single

You may desperately want to be married, but if you're single, embrace it! Enjoy your singledom while you have it. It's much more attractive to see a single woman loving her life and not sulking around, complaining that there aren't any good men around. You don't want to seem so independent that you don't need or want a man, but do seem engaged in your life and happy in general with your status.

If you are just coming out of a relationship, commit to yourself that you will never get involved with the wrong type of guy again—no more bad boys, no more jerks, no more emotionally-unavailables, no more dreamers and jobless-Joes, no more Peter Pans and Momma's Boys. No more wasting time with guys who don't deserve you! It's time to make this promise to yourself and make better choices that will get you what you ultimately want. And until you meet Mr. Right, enjoy being single by doing nice things for yourself: take bubble baths, cook gourmet dinners just for you, go to the movies alone, and read lots of books. Look at it as though you are building a solid relationship with *yourself* that will serve you for the rest of your life.

STEP 4: BE OF SERVICE

Nothing will get you out of yourself and dissipate any level of unhappiness than being of service. I know you're busy and barely have time to do anything for yourself, much less someone else, but it is definitely worth the effort. If you already have service commitments, then great. If not, think about what you love to do—what are you passionate about? You could volunteer at the local animal shelter, or donate money every month to a third world country. On a small scale, offer to help your friend who is going out of town with dog-sitting or watering her plants. Anything to help others will do. Not only will this enrich your life, and the lives of those you serve, but men will notice this about you and it will be one of the key factors in him falling for you. This isn't the primary reason you're doing it, but it is one of the benefits.

STEP 5: MAKE AMENDS

We all have relationships that teach us lessons. Undoubtedly there are people who have hurt you, and those whom you have hurt. Go to the ones you have hurt and make amends. Don't worry about whether or not they apologize to you, just clean up your side of the street. Forgive easily, take responsibility, and move on. Clean it all up so that you have a clean slate and good, healthy relationships with everyone you know. Obviously, some situations are more complicated and it may not be so simple and easy. But do what you can. If you need to enlist the help of a good therapist, then do it and pour your whole self into it. You are preparing for the man of your dreams, so be thorough!

STEP 6: CLEAN UP YOUR LIFE

When I say "clean up your life" I literally mean clean up your life. Is your apartment a mess? How about your car? If your home and car are disasters then it will reflect on you. You can't avoid having men in your apartment forever. Eventually they will know that you're trying to hide something. If you're something of a hoarder, take one section of each room and begin organizing and throwing stuff out. Streamline your life. Make room for him. And then add some nice touches: fresh flowers on the table, make your bed everyday, light some candles. Show men that you have a feminine touch and that your home matters to you. You don't have to be Martha Stewart, but do show that you care about such things.

STEP 7: AVOID SITUATIONS THAT UNDERMINE SELF-ESTEEM

If you have had a pattern of getting involved in situations that are not good for your self-esteem, make a decision now to end that cycle. Just make the decision, that from now on, you will make healthier choices and you will not allow any negativity into your life. Maybe you need to weed out some people who aren't good for you. Maybe you need to stop going to events or places that aren't good for you. You know which situations and people help to build your self-confidence, and which ones don't. Embark upon a new path today by promising yourself that you will avoid anything negative and accept only that which builds you up. For example, if you have trouble being around certain people because you feel extremely insecure around them and feel unable to be your best self—avoid them until you feel stronger. Just go where the love is.

STEP 8: PRACTICE SELF-KINDNESS

Are you hard on yourself? Do you ever put yourself down, or have such high expectations for yourself that you are like a critical parent? If so, stop it! Stop being so tough and start showing yourself some love and kindness. Give yourself a break. Lighten up and look for the good in you. Learn to love and appreciate the qualities that are uniquely yours: your unique laugh, your pretty eyes, your sparkling personality, your talents, and so on. We all have plenty of strengths and a few weaknesses. Focus on your strengths. Forgive yourself of the mistakes you've made. The past is over and done. All we have is right now. Learn to be present in the Now and you'll realize that all is well. If you catch yourself being critical of yourself, stop and turn it around by thinking about what is positive about you.

STEP 9: SHOW GRATITUDE

I can think of nothing more powerful than an attitude of gratitude. It can transform your day, from a negative one to a positive one. Focus on what is good and right in your life and express to the Universe your profound gratitude, and the Universe will continue to send you positive things in return. It really works! Imagine how men will view you if you have a grateful attitude in general. If you are grateful for your life, your job, your relationships, your home, your pets, your family, his company—it's attractive! And the opposite is very unattractive: a lack of gratitude shows in your countenance, your face, your posture, your eyes. An ungrateful person seems dour, unhappy, and with a chip on her shoulder. It's a choice because there are always things for which you can be grateful. Make a list of the things you're grateful for and then carry that attitude with you throughout your day. You will attract more good things as you do so.

STEP 10: TAKE CARE OF YOURSELF

Good self-esteem is a natural by-product of taking good care of yourself. It all starts with good hygiene. If you are clean, smell fresh, dress nicely, have fresh breath, and the like, you are going to be perceived as someone with good self-esteem, and men are going to be very attracted to you. At some point the grunge look took over and ever since then you see women everywhere dressed like rag-a-muffins. It's not a good look ladies! I am all for being comfortable, but it becomes ridiculous. Put a little effort into your look—it will pay off, I promise. You will stand out and men will notice. Wear feminine dresses once in awhile, or bright colors that enhance your coloring. Look polished and classy. A big smile is the most attractive accessory you have so wear it often! And don't wear too much make up—wear just enough to bring out your beautiful traits, such as your eyes, smile, and glowing skin. Also, make exercise a regular part of your life. I know it's really hard—but you want to have a toned, healthy body. A healthful, water-based diet goes without saying.

I know I'm not telling you anything you don't already know...but hopefully just reading the words will inspire you to get on track if you've let yourself go at all. Go out and buy yourself a new work-out outfit and/or running shoes, start an exercise journal and establish some specific goals, map out your diet menu for the next six weeks—anything to get you excited about a new level of health and vitality.

Be True to Yourself

And last but not least, high self-esteem comes from living in accordance with your own values—in other words, being true to yourself. You *earn* your high self-esteem through making wise choices in your life. When you live in accordance with your values you begin to feel good about yourself and your self-concept improves. When you go against your values, your self-esteem drops. You begin to feel poorly about yourself, and it shows.

As I've mentioned before, listening to your inner voice is so important. It takes practice to recognize it but if you ask yourself, "What does my heart tell me to do?" the answers will come. You will feel a peaceful clarity about the situation.

As you are true to yourself, and you establish new values as a result of reading this book perhaps—you will become clear as to what you will or will not accept in your life. This could mean not allowing another person to abuse you ever again. It could mean never allowing yourself to get involved with men you know are unhealthy or emotionally unavailable. You will begin to practice new behaviors. This could mean not calling men anymore, or saying no to heavy make-out sessions when it's too soon.

As your self-esteem grows, not only will you like yourself more, but you'll begin to feel more worthy of a high-quality man who will cherish you. Your low self-esteem undoubtedly played a role in you having sex too soon in the past. Now it's time for your *internal voice* to decide for you when the time is right (as well as a clear head).

Aside from high self-esteem, there are many qualities that men find particularly appealing... this is the subject of chapter 12.

Chapter 12
The Ten Qualities Men Find Most Irresistible in a Lifetime Mate

Since men are the natural pursuers it only makes sense that women need to be as attractive as possible in order to capture their interest. But we all know that appearances only go so far and that what may *initially* attract men may not necessarily *sustain* their interest. Some women seem to have some magical quality that draws men to them like magnets. They never lack for dates, and everywhere they go, men take notice. If you are one of those women, good for you! You have an advantage in the dating world. But maybe you're not so fortunate and attracting men has been a challenge for you. Rest assured, you will find a lot of helpful information in these pages that will transform your dating life. But don't be one of those women who says, "Hey, if guys don't like me as I am, then too bad." I am not suggesting that you become someone other than yourself, or to be fake in any way. I just want you to be the best you can be, and to be open to learning about how men think and how they view women. If you aren't naturally charming and vivacious, is it so terrible to work at improving yourself? It all boils down to what it is you want, and how much effort you are willing to put into getting it. Hopefully you won't have much work to do!

THE 10 QUALITIES MEN FIND MOST IRRESISTABLE IN A LIFETIME MATE

1. **ATTRACTIVE**. We all know that looks aren't everything and there are plenty of women who aren't gorgeous who get men to love them. However, in general, men are very visual and they want a woman who is attractive to them. They have to see you as visually appealing in order to get excited about approaching you. Once he approaches, you can win him over with your winning personality, but to draw him to you, you will want to be as attractive as possible.

2. **INNER HAPPINESS.** Men appreciate a woman who is happy and who has a sense of gratitude for what she has and where she's at in life. This makes sense when we consider the opposite, which would be a moody, depressed, and melancholy woman. Men often feel responsible when we are unhappy—they think *they* aren't able to make us happy, and that is incredibly frustrating for them. But inner happiness is our own responsibility and we have to do whatever we can to find it for ourselves. I really believe that as you implement the concepts in this book, you will be happier than ever.

3. **STRENGTH OF CHARACTER**. A person's character refers to their combined moral or ethical structure. Some of the qualities that strengthen character are honesty, integrity, loyalty, patience, tolerance, humility, trustworthiness, and unselfishness. Having good character means having control over yourself and being in command of your life and choices. It's about having the courage to make wise choices, and showing compassion and tolerance for others as well. You want to strive to reach your own personal goals, but never at the expense of others. You are a trustworthy, honest, thoughtful person who can be counted on. Loyalty is a huge one for men. They want to know that they can totally trust the woman they love. Do a reality check and see if there are any areas you can work on in this department.

4. **HEALTHFULNESS**. We talked about this in the previous chapter. Men love vivacious women who exude healthfulness. When you're healthy you shine. You glow. You light up from within and look refreshed, never haggard. When your diet is right your eyes sparkle and your hair shines. Your skin looks clear and fresh. These are signs of youthfulness, so no matter what your age, if you're taking care of yourself, you'll shine and it will show.

5. **FEMININITY**. In her book *Being a Woman*, Dr. Toni Grant describes the ideal woman by describing the "Madonna" and "Courtesan" aspects of the feminine personality. The Madonna is the spiritual and inspirational side; the Courtesan is the playful, sensual side. Grant writes, "The woman who embraces both the Madonna and Courtesan aspects of feminine personality is irresistible to men. Her Madonna is idealistic and unattainable; her Courtesan is visceral and enticing. Utilizing these two powerful aspects of femininity, women civilize and domesticate men, channel their sexual energies, and inspire them to greatness."

Femininity is more than just being female. It is a *way of being*. It is a certain softness, gentleness, and tenderness within a woman's nature. This quality can be seen in her appearance, movements, voice, and manner. Femininity is the opposite of masculinity, which is typically more aggressive, harsh, tough, and loud. Being a truly feminine woman will attract more men to you than anything else. *Men are magnetized by feminine women.* They are fascinated, intrigued, inspired, and amused by the feminine creature who is so clearly different than they are. The feminine quality instantly awakens the chivalrous, manly qualities in him.

When a man is in the presence of a woman who is not in touch with her feminine side, he sees her as just a person and will treat her accordingly. He will most likely be cordial and friendly, but his instincts of wanting to protect, cherish, and adore won't be awakened. You want to be viewed as a very feminine woman who can comfortably hang out with men, but you don't want to be viewed as "one of the guys."

How to Bring Out Your Feminine Side

In bringing out your feminine side, the key lies in the way you look, feel, smell, talk, walk, and act. Take a look at women who seem to epitomize this. They seem to love being women. They wear feminine clothing such as dresses, skirts, flowered prints, hats, ruffles. They wear perfume (don't overdo it!). They speak in a soft voice; they aren't loud, boisterous, or obnoxious. They have a gracious, calm spirit about them. The following are definitions of some of the qualities that make up a truly feminine woman:

Gracious: Marked by kindness and courtesy. Marked by tact and delicacy. Merciful, compassionate. Characterized by elegance and good taste.

Dignified: Esteemed or honored. Showing poise and self-respect.

Serene: Unruffled, tranquil. Unclouded.

Peaceful: Undisturbed by strife, turmoil, or disagreement. Tranquil. Opposed to strife.

6. **PLAYFULNESS**. Men go crazy for playfulness. This quality charms men and sweeps away some of their seriousness. It's a great way to lighten his mood and bring out *his* more playful side. Part of having a playful attitude is having spunk. If you only develop the sweeter, kinder side of yourself without having some fire or backbone, you can appear to be too docile or submissive.

Justin, 38, shared this with me: I need a woman who won't let me take advantage of her. It isn't that I want to take advantage, but if I know I can get away with it, I don't treat her as well. I guess it's human nature. I like a woman who will put me in my place if that's what I need.

Another perspective comes from Joey, 29: A woman who is a bit feisty is very intriguing. If she's just too nice or easy-going, I find her a little on the boring side. But a woman with spunk is exciting. She can take it too far of course, but just the right amount is very attractive.

Spunk comes from having confidence and not being easily controlled. When you have this quality, you feel free to say what's on your mind without apology or explanation. You aren't rude or blunt in a way that offends people, but in a playful and innocent way you speak your mind and are not constantly trying to people-please or acquiesce.

Playfulness and spunk are childlike qualities. Not only are they appealing to men, but they are excellent ways to express ourselves to men without alienating them. In describing these qualities in little girls, Helen Andelin, author of *Fascinating Womanhood* writes:

They are so trusting, so sincere, and so innocent, and yet so piquant and outspoken that they are often teased into anger. They are too innocent to feel hate, jealousy, resentment, and the uglier emotions. When such a child is teased, she does not respond with some hideous sarcasm. Instead, she stamps her foot and shakes her curls and pouts. She gets adorably angry at herself because her efforts to respond are impotent.

How do others, especially men, respond to this type of behavior? Mrs. Andelin writes, "We feel an irresistible longing to pick up such a child and hug it. We would do anything rather than permit such an adorable little thing to suffer danger or want; to protect and care for such a delightfully human little creature would be nothing less than a delight. This is much the same feeling that a woman inspires in a man when she expresses anger in a childlike way. Her ridiculous exaggeration of manner makes him suddenly want to laugh; makes him feel, in contrast, stronger, more sensible and more of a man. This is why women who are little spitfires—independent and saucy—are often sought after by men. This anger, however, must be the sauciness of a child, and not the intractable stubbornness of a woman well able to "kill her own snakes".

Some of you reading this may cringe at this notion, but why not give this behavior a try and see for yourself how men respond? I think it's important to develop and use your childlike side, not as a way to manipulate or change a man, or to be fake and silly—but rather, to give you a way to express your feelings. This is much better than suppressing them, and you probably know from experience that expressing intense feelings of anger, resentment, and bitterness never works—it only destroys love. Childlike qualities bring out feelings of love and tenderness in a man and brings a couple closer together. It should definitely be in your little bag of behaviors that help to enhance a relationship.

7. **NURTURING/LOVING.** Men need to know that the woman they marry has a nurturing, caring nature (especially if they want children). Barry, 54, described how much he appreciated this trait in his wife:

When my wife and I were first dating, I had the opportunity of seeing her interact with her nieces and nephews. I've always been mesmerized by how loving and kind she is with them. They just love her, and I can see why. She never loses her patience, she just knows how to make them feel special. In fact, she's that way with everyone, which is partly why I fell in love with her. How could I resist someone so good?

Becoming a more loving woman requires finding ways to show people that you care. It means listening patiently when others are in need of an understanding friend. It means giving our time and attention. We become more loving as we let go of resentments and learn to forgive others. As we let go of old anger, worry, and fear, our hearts and souls expand and we are better able to give and receive love. Equally important, as our self-esteem improves, so does our capacity to love.

8. **RESPONSIBLE/RELIABLE.** This could be considered part of having strong character, but I felt it could stand on its own. So many people today are flaky. Think about how many people in your life, just in this past week, have not returned calls/emails/texts, or who change plans, or contractors who didn't show up on time or at all... it really has become so common-place. But men don't want to marry women who are irresponsible and unreliable. Responsibility means following through with promises, being on time, and doing what needs to be done on a daily basis, especially those things you say

you're going to do. I used to know a woman who was always in debt, who was afraid of answering the phone because it might be a creditor. Unopened bills were lying around her apartment for months. She didn't even look at them! Yet she wouldn't think twice about going out and buying a whole new outfit.

Mark, 42, has had his fair share of flaky women, "I don't know what it is, but I keep attracting women who can't seem to get it together. My last girlfriend was constantly late. Her car was always out of gas and breaking down because she didn't handle the maintenance. If I asked her to do me a favor, she invariably forgot. I just couldn't count on her. It made me crazy! I couldn't imagine being married to her. She'd probably forget to feed the kids!"

A responsible woman is *able to deal with problems*. Life is full of tragedies and sudden changes that can throw you off kilter emotionally. While a man appreciates a woman who needs him and his masculine protection, he also wants her to show strength and courage when a crisis occurs. He likes to know that she can rise to the occasion, rather than fall apart.

Being responsible means being organized. Create a budget for yourself, set up a filing system, keep track of appointments in a day planner, and set daily/weekly/monthly goals.

Being self-disciplined is yet another part of being responsible. Very few people are perfectly self-disciplined. We procrastinate and avoid doing certain things, such as exercising, dieting, or quitting smoking. It's very hard to be disciplined, but it's worth it. Make a list of the things you need to change in your life and vow to start over.

Being able to not have sex until it's right is a good sign that you're a disciplined woman. Men take those things into account, even though they may never voice their thoughts. It's also important to be disciplined in showing up for work, paying bills, staying in shape, avoiding overindulging, and maintaining balance in general.

9. **FLEXIBILITY.** Men especially appreciate women who can be flexible. Don't get me wrong—men enjoy women with opinions and who speak their minds—but it's when they absolutely *oppose* their way of thinking or plans they make, without ever showing flexibility, that they have a problem. Especially on the first few dates, you don't want to be combative or too argumentative. Do you want to be "right" or do you want a boyfriend? Do you want to have fun and be light, or do you want to create bad vibes for the evening? Lighten up and let things roll off your back. Go with the flow. Have a good attitude. Say things like, "I guess we can agree to disagree" with a sweet smile.

10. **VULNERABILITY.** I have asked men what one quality in a woman has the greatest impact on them. Remarkably, I hear the same answer over and over again: vulnerability. There is something appealing about this quality for a man. It brings out his protective side. He feels she *needs* him. It also makes him feel invincible. On the other hand, men don't want a *needy* woman. There is an art to balancing vulnerability with strength, but once mastered, you will definitely stand out as special and unique in men's eyes. Marilyn Monroe is the best example of female vulnerability. Men were crazy for her and it was primarily because of her vulnerability. Men felt an overwhelming desire to take care of her and protect her when in her presence. She obviously had problems in other areas of her life, but we can't ignore the incredible attraction that men all over the world had for her.

Some women today see being vulnerable as a serious weakness, and maybe it is in the business world. But when it comes to love, the rules change. The opposite of being vulnerable is to be in total control without needing anyone else. Men may *respect* that in a person, but they won't necessarily be attracted to it in a romantic sense. They may even get turned off. I once watched a couple shopping in the mall. The woman was carrying a very large bag filled with merchandise from one of the department stores. Her boyfriend was trying to get her to give him the bag to carry, because it was so heavy. She vehemently refused. Although they were wrestling with it in a playful sort of way, this woman made it very clear that she didn't need his help—she could do just fine on her own. Maybe she could in that particular instance, but she missed out on a wonderful opportunity to let him come to her aid. It is these small, brief moments that make men feel needed and that enhance a relationship.

Contrary to popular belief, we do need men. We don't need them to validate us as worthy human beings or to be responsible for our happiness, but we do need them. They offer physical protection. Many men have excellent problem-solving skills. You probably do as well, but it's nice to have another perspective. And men also offer companionship, love, someone with whom to grow old. I suggest you start looking at the qualities you appreciate in a man and start allowing yourself to relax and be vulnerable enough for him to utilize some of those strengths.

At first glance the items on this list may seem old-fashioned and dated. The list is based on many years of personal experience with dating and getting to know men and how they respond to different behaviors and traits, as well as my observations of others and the countless interviews I have conducted with men and women. Obviously the list isn't exhaustive or set in stone. Most men love a great sense of humor, but it isn't something that is absolutely necessary for most men. Many men love a strong woman with strong opinions—and I believe that a woman with integrity, who is happy and responsible, is most likely that type of woman. But these are the traits that I have seen that really *move* men.

The point of this book is to help you develop deep, lasting love based on a solid commitment—these are the traits that I believe elicit deep feelings of love in a man and that will lead him to want to spend the rest of his life with you. I am not saying you need to be perfect so that a man will want and love you. Men don't want a "perfect" woman—they want a woman who is authentically herself and they expect flaws. But look at the list and see if you possess some of these qualities, and see if there are some traits you may need to work on a bit. Don't be too stubborn to take a stab at self-improvement for the sake of love!

Chapter 13
Getting a Marriage Proposal

Getting a man to propose is not as difficult as it may seem. If you have followed the steps outlined in this book, the proposal will come naturally and easily. You started the ball rolling in the right direction when you had the Pre Sex Pow-Wow. Part of that discussion was that marriage would be the goal. To review, you said something like:

"I'm only interested in having sex with someone who loves me and wants a real relationship—based on love, commitment, trust, and respect. I want to know that we have the same goals for the relationship. I don't want to waste time—mine or yours. I want sex to *add* to the relationship—not be the main attraction."

A conversation then ensues and you discuss the parameters of the relationship… you will be sexually exclusive and won't date other people, you are a real couple in love and marriage is the goal (if that's what you want). I also suggested that you mark a date in your calendar. This is a date you both agree on—it's the date on which you reconvene to further the discussion. Either you get engaged on or around that date, or you decide to postpone it, or you break up. Most men won't have a hard time with this, if they want you. Just put it this way:

"I think we should pick a date—say, 9 months from now—and that's the date we either get engaged or decide it isn't working. There's no reason why we can't figure out whether or not we want to marry each other within 9 months (or 1 year, or whatever time frame you prefer). I don't want to get into a relationship that drags on for months and then years. That's not for me."

If he won't go for it, then accept his answer and sweetly say:

"Okay, I understand. You're not comfortable with setting a date. So, let's just take it slow and see what happens. I'm in no hurry. I just want you to know that if we are going to be in a *sexual* relationship, I need to know that we are working towards marriage and that we have the same time-frame in mind."

Does this type of conversation terrify you? It shouldn't. You are absolutely within your right to discuss the most important points related to the relationship you can make. No one else is going to set you up—it's all up to you! If he has the right to ask for your body, time, heart, and everything else that goes with all of that, then you most certainly have the right to discuss what your expectations are, what you want (both short and long term), and how you see it all playing out. But the key is that all of these things need to be discussed and locked down *before* sex. Love comes before sex, and so do all of the practical details—such as where is this going, what do we want, how are we going forward, what do you mean to me, and so on.

I promise you, it isn't too much to ask. I personally think it's too much to ask a girl to make available her most intimate parts on the first few dates! Something is wrong with that picture, right? Let's get your priorities straight and move forward with confidence.

Chapter 13 Getting A Marriage Proposal

What Not to Do

First, let me say that you never want to ask for a marriage proposal directly, or hint, or try to talk him into it. This is all beneath you. You never have to beg for marriage. He should be knocking down your door, practically begging *you* to marry *him*! Like I said, if you're following everything in the book, it will most likely come along naturally. However, even the most skilled women can find themselves in a pickle, whereby the proposal isn't forthcoming. Sometimes you need a little help and he needs a little nudge…all without him ever knowing you had anything to do with it.

Please keep in mind that all of these concepts are applied *only once he is already in love with you*, and it is only a matter of outside obstacles that stand in the way of him proposing.

1) **Discuss your original date you set and determine where you are.** When he made the first sexual advance and you had the Pre Sex Pow-Wow, you established a date in which you would either get engaged, or postpone the date, or break up. If you reach that date and he's still hemming and hawing, then have a sit-down discussion and see what his issues are with moving forward. Try to apply the concepts in this section and help him overcome those obstacles. Explain to him that this was the agreement, and that although you don't want to ever pressure him, you will have to move on if he knows he doesn't want to marry you. This isn't an ultimatum because this was established by the two of you months ago.

2) **Make it difficult for him not to propose.** During the first few months in particular, you want to be on your very best behavior. This doesn't mean you should slack off and be a schlump once you have him hooked—no, no, no. You just

want to put forth extra effort while he's considering the pros and cons of tying the knot with you. So, during this time you look your best, smell your prettiest, and behave with your best foot forward. You want him to see how amazing and stellar your character is, what a fabulous cook and homemaker you are, how unselfish and kind you are with your friends, family, and the less fortunate. He should have no reason whatsoever *not* to propose. Kick it all up a notch and be a shining star. Have a fabulous attitude, show gratitude for him and all that he does, be a lover of life and let him see what an amazing woman you truly are. He'll take notice and at some point, he will realize that losing you would be the worst thing that could ever happen to him.

3) **Help him overcome any doubts or obstacles.** Men like to have things in order before they move forward with the huge decision to get married. If they aren't finished with school, for example, or their finances aren't in order, they may balk at the idea of moving forward. Maybe he's afraid to ask you for some reason, or he doesn't feel he can afford to give you the lifestyle you want. Your part is to be the supportive girlfriend who helps him overcome each and every doubt or obstacle. Paint a picture for him of how it *could* be… in other words, help him overcome the obstacles by giving him a visual of how it all could work out. This is simply a conversation, in which you are building him up, and letting him know that you believe in him and in his ability to make it all happen. You know he will be successful, and that together you can do anything. You make it clear that you are a *team*, and that with your support he will be able to accomplish all that he wants to accomplish. Convince him that all you want is him and that together you can do anything.

4) ***Get him to confide in you and develop a strong trust and bond.*** You want him to turn to you with his thoughts, feelings, concerns, and so on. He should feel that you are his true confidant—the one he trusts above all else with his deepest thoughts, and even insecurities. Be a great listener, but don't offer advice or try to be his counselor. You are simply his partner in life and a compassionate sounding board for him. The best thing you can tell him is, "I know you're going to do/be great. I believe in you." He needs to know that you are behind him no matter what, on his side, cheering and rooting for him. He doesn't want you to try to fix or solve his problems, or to point out what he needs to be doing differently. And never, ever use another man as a shining example. Just listen, be supportive and encouraging. That's it. Over time, it is only you that he will want to go to and he'll feel that you are irreplaceable and indispensable.

5) ***Create romantic situations that are conducive to a proposal.*** Be sure to create an environment that might elicit a proposal. Have him over for a candlelight dinner with soft music. Plan a big trip that could be the perfect time and place for such an occasion. If your birthday is coming up, or Valentine's Day, be sure and create a setting that would be perfect for him to pop the question. Try not to be too disappointed if he doesn't, and don't be obvious about your intention, but make sure the situation is ripe for a proposal. Make it easy for him to propose.

6) ***Create an Emergency.*** This may seem extreme and even a bit far-fetched, but how badly do you want to get engaged? If a man is dragging his feet and you've tried everything else, you may have to create an emergency situation that causes him to realize that if he doesn't act, he will lose you. Moving to a new location is the best way to create this type of situation.

Love Before Sex

And maybe moving to a new city would be a great thing for you to do. In any case, tell him you're considering relocating, and make sure it's far away. Watch his reaction. He will realize that he would have to step up to the plate in order to not lose you. If you are sitting there, willing to wait forever for him, and be available for as long as he wants, then he won't be as motivated to act. But if you say, "I'm thinking about moving to Colorado or New York... which one do you think would be best for me?" he is forced to consider whether or not he could live without you. If he really loves you, the thought of losing you will drive him crazy and he will tell you to forget about the crazy idea of moving because you need to stay there and marry him. But if he says, "Well, New York is nice" then you also have your answer.

7) **End the relationship.** I know this seems harsh, and it would be the last resort, but sometimes it is the only answer. Some men are just tough and they resist marriage until they have no other option. Losing you would be the worst thing for him, and if he really loves you he knows that. Like I said, you aren't giving him an ultimatum... you are saying, "Look, I love you very much and this saddens me greatly, but I have to move on. It seems obvious that you don't want the same thing I do, and that's okay, it's just that I can't continue in a situation where my needs aren't met. We discussed what we wanted from the beginning, and we are now at a place where we need to move to the next level, and I can see that you are resisting that. I don't want to pressure you or give you an ultimatum, so there's only one thing for me to do, and that's move on." And then you leave immediately. On the way out the door, hopefully, he will grab you and say, "No, I won't let you go. I love you so much. I do want to marry you and I will marry you." It's a risk, yes. But it's worth it because you then get the big prize, versus settling for something so

inferior, whether it is now or later (possibly with someone new). You wouldn't be happy being stuck in a dead-end situation that never leads to marriage, or that takes years to get there. So gather all of your courage and do the right thing.

What is Your Goal?

Perhaps marriage isn't your goal. It doesn't have to be—in today's world we have the luxury and freedom to tailor our relationships to suit our needs. And with the divorce rate what it is, we can't say that marriage is necessarily the ideal way to go. It isn't for everyone. Maybe you want to be in love, monogamous, and loyal to one person for the rest of your life, but without the marriage certificate. That's up to you. I do believe that the legality of marriage adds a level of commitment and surrender that can make the relationship more rock solid—and yet not necessarily. So, think about what kind of relationship you want and be very clear about it before you start dating because you need to know what you want before that sexual advance comes around. You'll want to be prepared to know what to ask for and to be able to establish the parameters for the relationship.

Be Patient

Sometimes love is slow to grow. This is a very delicate and complicated process and you may not know everything that is going on in your man's life that could be holding him back. If you know he loves you, you have a good relationship, and you had a solid Pow-Wow, then just continue to be your radiant, joyful self and be patient. Men like to move at their own pace and feel like it is their idea to propose, so hang in there if it feels right. But do have a time frame in mind, just so things don't drag on for years.

Your chances of winning over the man of your choice are very high if you follow everything in this book. He will find you completely charming, adorable, effervescent, and fascinating, and he will want to have you in his life forever. Be patient, but also confident in yourself and in the fact that you know you're an amazing catch. Hold your head high, and carry yourself with the utmost dignity, knowing that a proposal is forthcoming, and that he will be extremely lucky for you to say *yes*.

Chapter 14

The Ten Most Common Mistakes Women Make

After working with many women, I have discovered some very clear patterns in the choices they make. Following are the most common mistakes women make.

Mistake #1: They Go Out With Men Who Are Wrong For Them

This is probably the most common mistake of all. As they say, love is blind. But sometimes a feeling is not love at all. It could be lust, a weak moment, loneliness, or timing. Maybe you liked his eyes or the way he danced. Maybe he said all the right things. Whatever the reasons, many women don't take the time required to learn the important things about a man before becoming sexual with him. They end up getting physical, and then a year or so later they find themselves going through another breakup.

Sometimes getting serious with Mr. Wrong can cost you a lot more than time. No one knows this better than Susan, 56.

"The most devastating relationship for me was with a man I met several years ago. We had sex fairly soon, and I ended up getting pregnant. In those days you got married. He asked me to marry him, I quit my job, and we made plans for the wedding. Then he announced to me one day that he couldn't marry me because the girl back in his hometown was also pregnant. I couldn't believe it! Here I was planning on marrying this man, constantly thinking about it, feeling good about the fact that our baby would have two parents and then he changes his mind about marrying me. And he is with another woman to boot! I was so traumatized, I didn't know what to do. I was deeply wounded. I sometimes wonder if I'll ever be able to trust again."

"I had an abortion. I still haven't been able to forgive myself for that decision. I know I've got to let go, but it's not easy. I feel it also contributed to even more self-esteem problems. I felt unworthy of love. After the abortion, I got on the Pill and began sleeping with a lot of different men. I just didn't care anymore. I felt like I was a slut because of what I had done and because he left me. I couldn't possibly be worth much, right? A whole vicious cycle was created that has been extremely difficult to end.

"I found myself attracting men who were abusive because of how horrible I felt about myself. That's the only reason I was able to sleep with men I barely knew and who didn't love me. Since I didn't care about myself, why should they?

"I gave sex to get love. Even though I essentially enjoy the physical act of sex, I primarily did it to feel loved. When I look back on my past relationships, I realize that it usually wasn't love I was receiving, but at the time, I wanted to believe it so badly that I suppose I convinced myself it was love.

"I hate to admit it, but I have settled for very little in my relationships. Sex has connected me so strongly to men that I have convinced myself that I was in love with them when I really wasn't. We had no connection outside of the bedroom. Through sex, we were able to avoid being honest with each other and avoid talking about what really mattered. But you can't stay in bed all the time."

You May Have a Pattern of Getting Involved with the Wrong Men If:

- You find yourself losing respect for him.
- You do not appreciate his values, the way he conducts himself, or his thoughts and opinions.
- You fight over silly, little things that normally would not bother you.
- You often find yourself irritated with him.
- You find you have very little in common outside of the bedroom.

You Ignore the Red Flags

In most relationships men will give out clues, signals, or even direct statements about who they are and what they are willing to give. One divorced woman I know told me that her ex-husband once said, "Hey, you knew I was an asshole when you were dating me." She honestly thought he would never be that way *with her*, so she ended up marrying him. But it was only a matter of time. Now she's dealing with him as an ex-husband, and he makes her life hell. The sad reality is that he did show his true colors early on—she just ignored the signs. She rationalized, justified, and minimized his behavior. Why? Because she wanted to see the good in him. She didn't want to be too judgmental. And he was a good-looking guy who paid her attention. At the time, that was very seductive to her.

Ask Yourself These Questions in the Early Stages of Dating

- Does this person want the same things I want in life?
- Is this person ready for a serious relationship?
- Is he a nice person?
- Do I like this man?
- Does he have integrity?

Mistake #2: They Don't Know What Their Standards/Values Are

It seems that most women today are more sexually aggressive than ever before, and they don't have clear boundaries and standards that they live by. But we all have conditions. Conditions are a part of almost everything we do. Before being hired for a job, you are required to prove your worthiness. When you go to a restaurant, you are required to pay the bill and behave in a civilized manner in order to avoid being thrown out. Before accepting you into their buildings, landlords can require a credit check, a security deposit, and references. When you go to the bank for a loan, they don't just hand over the money because you are cute or you look trustworthy!

Why would it be any different in relationships? In your case, your assets are your heart, feelings, and future. When you are willing to have sex without any kind of commitment or expression of love, you are essentially saying, "My conditions are not very stringent. You can have me without having to jump through any hoops at all. Have at it!"

Anna, 28, never gave her own standards much thought:

Chapter 14 The Ten Most Common Mistakes Women Make

"It is amazing, but I never considered that there should be any kind of discussion before having sex. I just figured I would do it when I'm ready. I thought that if you had sex early in the relationship, you could get it out of the way and then enjoy the relationship. We could relax, the pressure was off, and I didn't have to worry about it. Maybe that's why my relationships haven't worked out very well."

It isn't just the women who lose out with sex too soon. Lack of standards can actually harm your partner because you don't give him an opportunity to give to you. His motivation is lost because of your neediness (which is due to Oxytocin). He pulls away because he feels smothered, trapped, or just overwhelmed. As he pulls away, you usually get scared and try even harder by giving more, which is just the opposite of what you should do. The only solution at that point is to give less and allow him to also be the giver and pursuer in the relationship. Men cannot love and cherish a woman who is willing to give so much of herself—especially her body—without expecting love. *In order for him to fall in love, he needs to give of himself.*

You Need to Establish Standards for Yourself if You Say Things Like:

- I believe in having sex when it feels right.
- I think 5 dates, or two months (or any specific length of time) is a good length of time to wait.
- It's not my style to talk about commitment and things like that, before having sex.
- It's too much like game-playing.
- I will have sex with him when I just can't stand it any longer.

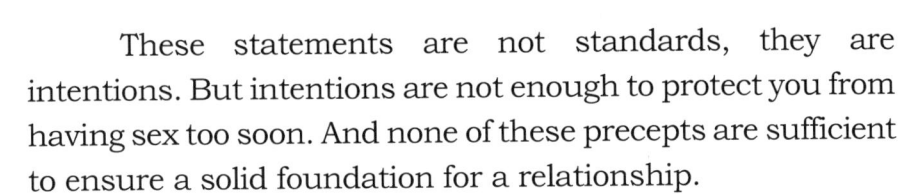

These statements are not standards, they are intentions. But intentions are not enough to protect you from having sex too soon. And none of these precepts are sufficient to ensure a solid foundation for a relationship.

Begin Establishing Standards By Asking Yourself These Questions

- Am I willing to have sex without a commitment?
- Do I need to be in love before being sexual? Does he need to be in love with me?
- How long will I have to know someone well enough to have sex with them?
- Would I prefer to wait until I am committed, engaged, or married?
- What is my Pre-sex Pow-Wow going to consist of (see chapter 3)?

Mistake #3: *They Don't Know What They Want*

If you don't know what you want, you may end up with something you wish you didn't have. In Anthony Robbin's book *Unlimited Power*, he writes, "When the mind has a defined target, it can focus and direct and refocus and redirect until it reaches its intended goal. If it doesn't have a defined target, its energy is squandered... knowing what you want determines what you will get. Before something happens in the *external* world, it must first happen in the *internal* world. There's something rather amazing about what happens when you get a clear internal representation of what you want. It programs your mind and body to achieve that goal."

Some people grow up never really thinking through what they want. They don't realize the number of options available to them. Some, on the other hand, know exactly what they want from the time they are very young. And everything seems to fall into place. But for most, it's a difficult, long process to decide what they want.

We are the sculptors, free to mold our lives into whatever we are inspired to create. Of course, we can receive inspiration from all kinds of sources: friends, family, books, school, movies, spirituality, and so on. If it's a lasting relationship you want, then you need to maintain that as your focus and take the necessary steps to make that happen. You may not be able to control when or how you will meet your mate, but you can do so much in the meantime. You can take better care of yourself and make room in your life for that person. The rest will work itself out. You'll draw it all to you when the time is right. When you remain focused on reaching your goal, and you are visualizing it, you create the opportunities and even the ability to achieve it.

Ask yourself: what is my dream? What am I passionate about? If you aren't sure what your talents are, look back on your childhood. What were you doing as a little girl? What came naturally to you? Find your purpose in life and strive to fulfill it.

In terms of relationships, I find that most women don't really know what they are capable of achieving. They have had so many negative experiences or have seen such little success in the relationships of others that they believe they won't ever have much more. Many women have never experienced what it feels like to be adored and cherished by a man. But I promise you, this kind of love is possible for us all. We all know at least one couple who has this kind of love, and if that's the case, we know it's possible for almost everyone.

Love Before Sex

Sometimes it's easier to figure out what you want by first determining what you *don't* want. Here are a few examples:

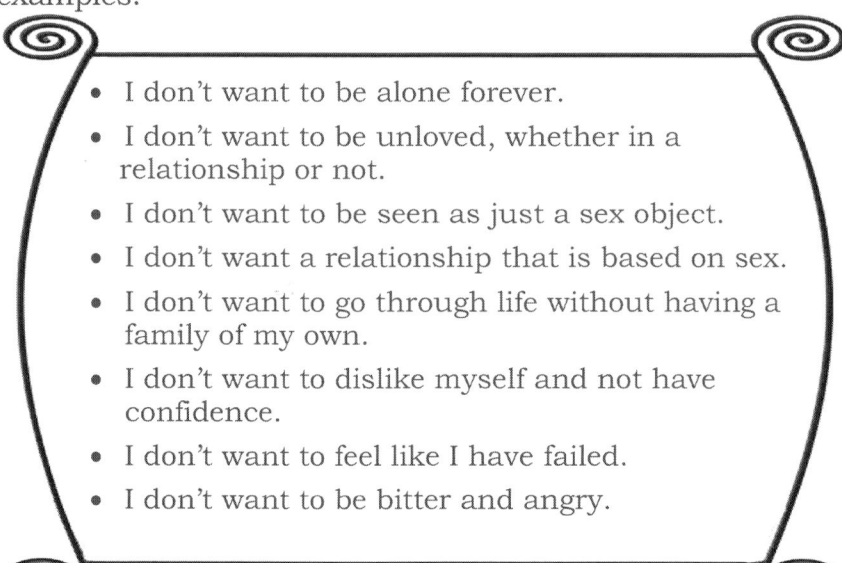

- I don't want to be alone forever.
- I don't want to be unloved, whether in a relationship or not.
- I don't want to be seen as just a sex object.
- I don't want a relationship that is based on sex.
- I don't want to go through life without having a family of my own.
- I don't want to dislike myself and not have confidence.
- I don't want to feel like I have failed.
- I don't want to be bitter and angry.

Take a fresh notebook or journal and find a quiet place where you can spend about an hour or so to contemplate what you want your life to be like. It doesn't matter what your age is. Look at the big picture first, then get more and more specific. Pick one aspect and write it at the top of the one page. For example, "Spiritual Goals." Then describe on that page what kind of person you want to be spiritually, and what type of spiritual practice you would like to implement. Don't worry about writing down specific goals yet—just write out a description of what you might be doing, how it looks, how it feels to you, where you are. Then take another page and write "Physical Goals" at the top and describe those on that page. Include your spiritual, physical, emotional, social, financial, and relationship goals, and add any other ones that come to mind.

On another page write, "The Kind of Marriage (or Relationship) I want." Describe what your day might look like, where you might live, the kinds of things you and your spouse might do, how many children you might have, how you treat each other, and what the general feeling is in the home. In chapter 9 you created a "Man Plan" and a "Relationship Map", so anything you come up with here can be added to that.

Your goals will undoubtedly change over time. It is important that you remain flexible, but it is very helpful to have a good idea of what you want or what you envision for yourself. By having this road map for your life, you will be well on your way to getting what you want.

Mistake #4: They Send Out the Wrong Messages

You may be saying you want to wait, but your body language and appearance may be saying something else. When you send out the message that you are ultra sexy, you usually end up getting the kind of attention that puts you in compromising positions. Don't be deceived into thinking that men want "sexy." Men may appreciate a sexy woman, but it is not a requirement for marriage. Men who are serious about finding a wife put qualities such as sweetness, loyalty, honesty, and understanding a lot higher on their list.

Charlotte, 44, was always looking for an intense attraction:

"I had a picture of what I wanted, but I never even came to close to having that. I said I wanted a nice guy who loved me, but I was trying to use my body to get him. I thought if I just lost ten pounds and put on a mini skirt, I would get the guy. What a lie! What I got instead was a venereal disease, two abortions, and lot of heartache.

It's not your body that men fall in love with. It is who you are and how you make them feel. By sending out the wrong messages, you receive the wrong result. Once you truly make a solid commitment to putting love before sex, it is important that you get your actions in alignment with your words. Not only will it be easier for you, but men will also appreciate it.

You cannot send the right messages if you don't know who you are. Jamie, 29, tried every person in the book to try to get men to love her and want her.

"I wanted *connection*. I usually felt *disconnected* so I used men to try to connect, to get me out of my pain, and to help create some motivation for myself. If he wanted a strong woman, I was strong. If he wanted a weak, submissive type, I would become that. The games I used to try to hook men rarely worked. My timing was always off. If I tried to come across like a sexy siren, he would be attracted to a real mousy type of girl and vice versa. It was a never-ending source of frustration."

If you are ready to attract a man with whom you can spend the rest of your life, then the best way to do that is to be aware of the messages you send out. You may need to drop the sexy siren image and begin thinking like a true companion. I am not saying that only women who dress conservatively get married. But most men want to be able to take the woman they love home to their families and feel comfortable. They want to marry a mate, a partner, a woman who obviously cares about what her appearance and actions say about her as a person.

Chapter 14 The Ten Most Common Mistakes Women Make

Do You Send Out the Wrong Messages? Ask Yourself:

- Do I wear low-cut blouses, tight shirts, extra-tight jeans, and very short dresses and skirts? If so, why do I dress this way? Is it because I enjoy the attention it brings me, or is it because I need the validation from men that I am attractive? Or both?

- Is the attention I receive from men healthy? Is it the kind of attention I ultimately want and appreciate? How do the men I attract treat me in general?

- Do I send out mixed messages? Do I say I want a healthy, long-lasting relationship yet come on to men like a seductress?

- Do I say I want to get married yet look more like I want to party?

Sexual Talk/Sexting

The dangers of engaging in sexual talk are significant—whether it be via talking on the phone, texting, emailing, or Skyping. You may not see what the big deal is; after all, you are only *talking*. But something very powerful happens when two people begin discussing sexual preferences, fantasies, and the like. You minds begin to focus on the words, and eventually your thoughts lead to action. I don't know too many men who are able to discuss these things without eventually making some pretty strong advances. If he is the one instigating the conversation, simply tell him you are uncomfortable having that kind of conversation. He may think you are a little uptight at first, but eventually, he will gain respect for you. He'll know that he has to treat you with respect in the future.

Note: Some discussion of your sexual preferences can be beneficial once you have established a committed, monogamous relationship, and especially if you have determined that you want to be married. Although I don't feel it's always necessary to do this, discussing these issues can help you determine sexual compatibility. But discussing them prematurely only invites sexual pressure and frustration.

Mistake #5: They Don't Consider the Consequences

Another mistake many women make is that they allow men—or the idea of romance—to sweep them off their feet. They don't think rationally, and then they discover it's harder to think clearly in the heat of the moment.

At times, you get caught up in fantasies rather than focusing on reality. Mary, 54, is a good example of this:

"I just loved the fact that Martin found me so sexually appealing. He was so verbally and physically demonstrative. It made me feel incredible. Over and over he would tell me how beautiful I was and how he craved me. It made me want to make love to him just so I could hear those wonderful praises. I knew how to drive him wild, and I loved the feeling it gave me. I felt in control. I felt appreciated, adored, validated. I think I became more addicted to that *feeling* than to Martin or the sex."

Mary was not focused on creating a solid relationship that lasts. She was caught up in fulfilling a craving or a need within herself. She didn't think about the short-lived effects, she was strictly in the moment.

In many areas of life, going with the flow and being in the moment is the way to go. But not when it comes to something as serious as when you have sex with someone. Be flexible in terms of where you go to dinner or which movie you see, but not when it comes to your values.

Before Getting Sexual, Consider These Questions

- How am I going to feel after we have sex? What about after a week has passed? Am I even able to know?

- What if I were to get pregnant by this person?

- Do I trust this man well enough to bond to him?

- Do I really love this person, or am I just "in lust" or infatuated?

- Am I doing this to fill a void or to get me out of the pain I am in right now?

- Am I doing this for the right reasons? What are they?

Mistake #6: They Allow Their Hormones to Get the Best of Them

Valerie, 46, is a "junkie" for the sexual gratification she gets from a man.

"It's so difficult to wait! I rarely meet someone I'm attracted to and so when I do, we have a few drinks, he's saying all the right things, then he's touching me, and I melt. The pace that men move at today, it seems like it would be impossible to wait for long!"

Valerie says she wants to get married and be in love, but after talking with her further, I discovered that she really does not want that. Not now anyway. She is not willing to do what it takes to make it happen. She still wants to believe that love will magically come about. Also worth mentioning is that drugs and alcohol obviously play a big role in couples having sex too soon. You lose control over yourself.

Sometimes it's not sex in particular that you're longing for. It's the closeness and affection. You just want to be held, to be touched, and to feel close to someone. However, you forget that the intimacy you may experience today may last only a very short time and could be preventing you from finding the man with whom you could share the rest of your life.

Sheila, 61, remained in sexual relationships that were not right for her:

"In many of my relationships sex seemed to make everything all right. Whenever we fought, rather than working through it, we made up by having sex. During sex, we were connected. We felt close and romantic. I felt whole and loved when we had sex. That feeling would last for a little while, but eventually, the emptiness returned."

All of my ex-boyfriends looked great to me in the beginning. They were all charming, handsome (I thought so anyway), and intelligent. But I was more in love with the *idea* of being in love than I was in love with them. At times the chemistry can be so strong and the level of romantic intrigue so high that we literally lose our logical minds. We don't think about the future or the consequences. We don't think through the fact that we will bond emotionally with these men. And if they end up not being right for us, we will have a very difficult time pulling away.

Trisha, 50, had never been promiscuous in her life, but she found out how difficult it is to keep her own hormones in check:

"One night when I was out dancing, I met an extremely handsome man who basically swept me off my

Chapter 14 The Ten Most Common Mistakes Women Make

feet. I mean, he was gorgeous! I had never met a man I was so attracted to. I quickly became infatuated with him. We danced all evening and eventually made our way back to my apartment. He had too far to drive and it was late, so I offered him my couch. Well, he kissed me and I thought I would melt. Then we sat on the couch. He began asking me about what I like sexually. I guess I said the right buzz words for him because he picked me up and began carrying me back to my room. I kept saying no, I didn't think this was a good idea, but to be perfectly honest, I really didn't mean what I was saying, not entirely anyway. My mind said no but my body said yes!

"We had a wonderful evening and the next morning I drove him to his car. He asked if I was going to go dancing that night and I said yes. Later that night I saw him making his way toward me and when he reached my table, he put his hand out as if to shake my hand! My heart sank. After what happened last night, he now wants to shake my hand? I chose to ignore that gesture and gave him a hug. We danced, but after awhile he disappeared. He never called. I left several messages, but he would not return them.

"I had never felt so stupid in my whole life. I knew I had been used, and mainly because I allowed my sexual desires to overrule my logic. I always had been in control before, but I had never met a man like this before either. Next time I will know better."

Sometimes you may have the best of intentions only to find yourself repeating the same mistakes. It can be a very painful situation. *The desire to be true to your values has to outweigh your temporary desire for sexual gratification.* You must keep in mind that one day you will be able to fulfill your sexual needs, but you don't want to

251

fulfill them now, at the expense of your happiness, health, and future.

Before Reacting to Your Sexual Desires, Ask Yourself These Questions:

- Do I really see a future with this man, or am I just reacting to my hormones?
- Do I find myself dwelling on sexual thoughts, which lead me to acting on them?
- Do I want to forfeit building this relationship on love and commitment in order to have a few minutes of pleasure?
- Am I putting myself in a situation where I can be swept off my feet—that is, lose control?

Mistake #7: They Become Impatient for Love to Grow

Everything is fast these days. Fast food, faxes, E-mail, Fed-Ex/UPS, tweeting, etc... You name it, you can get it almost instantly. But love takes its own sweet time. Usually it takes so long that you end up saying, "Oh, forget it!" You know it's too soon to be sexual or intimate, but you just want to get on with it and start being a couple. You cannot see waiting for months to build something solid. You somehow want to get into the express lane. But the process of falling in love, getting to know the other person deeply, developing trust, and sharing a variety of experiences, all takes a tremendous amount of time. Considering who we marry and the success of our marriages are two of the most important aspects of our lives, being patient is a small price to pay.

But then you might wonder if sometimes you are being selfish. You hate to see him feeling so sexually frustrated. You want to please him and give him what he wants. These are all very natural desires, and one day you will be able to fulfill them. You will be able to experience the beautiful pleasure of opening up your heart and surrendering to a man worthy of your love. But if it's too soon, you're giving too much and you'll most likely get hurt.

If you understand and apply the principles that awaken love, then you can be sure that love will grow. As with so many things in life, you can't rush natural processes. One night as I was lying in bed, I became very frustrated because I just couldn't fall asleep. I tossed and turned and tried to make myself fall asleep, but to no avail. Then the thought came to me, *I will eventually fall asleep. There is no doubt about it in my mind. It is inevitable.* I felt the inevitability of falling asleep was a great metaphor for so many things in life. There are just certain things we can count on happening—in due time. But no matter how hard we may try to hurry the process, we are just spinning our wheels. Love is much the same way. We can only do our part and then the result has to be left to the natural process that is taking place. By realizing and accepting the fact that I would eventually fall asleep, I was able to relax and embrace the moment. I fell asleep shortly thereafter, and I was no longer frustrated.

Are You Using Sex Merely to Advance the Relationship?

Ask Yourself the following Questions:

- Do I think that by having sex, the relationship will be stronger and more serious?
- Do I think he will love me more if I have sex with him?

- Do I want to have great sex or do I want a marriage partner? (By the way, you can have both, but not by putting the cart before the horse).
- Am I able to be alone, without a relationship and still be happy?

Mistake #8: They Get Scared They May Lose Him

A healthy, happy relationship is almost impossible if you are operating from fear. When you become so insecure about losing him that you are unable to be true to your own feelings, then how can you possibly have a solid relationship?

We discussed this earlier in the book, but if you lose a man because you won't have sex with him, then obviously he's not the right man for you. His priorities differ from yours. Being a companion and building a lasting relationship is not high on his list, not with you that is. That may be hard to accept, but you must move on. It is that simple. On the subject of abstaining, one woman I know made this comment: "There is no way men would ever put up with this! There are too many women who will give them what they want!" That's like saying, "Men don't really want to get married, so you might as well just live with them." You don't lower your standards to match those of other women. On the contrary, you choose your standards based on your true values and goals, and then you see who is wise enough and into you enough to rise to them.

It is true that there are plenty of women who will have sex early on. But the choices other women make shouldn't have anything to do with your own choices. Besides, it doesn't take long for most men not only to get very bored with casual sex, but also to experience the emptiness of a shallow relationship.

Having sex with a man does not necessarily keep him interested, no matter how good the sex is. It may keep him coming back for a time, but it doesn't necessarily keep him interested in you as a woman with whom he wants to build a life-long commitment. Men are not as interested in sex as many people tend to believe, or as they might appear to be. Studies have shown that sex is usually closer to the bottom of the list of priorities for men than at the top. It's just that men are instinctively aggressive in pursuing women sexually, especially when they have never had them before. That doesn't mean it is the most important thing for them.

Ask Yourself These Questions:

- Am I afraid that he won't be able to love me for me, without sex?
- Am I afraid that if I don't have sex with him, he will leave me?
- Do I sometimes feel as though all I have to offer is sex?
- Do I sometimes feel like he only sees me as a sex object?
- Do I place too much focus on the sexual part of a relationship rather than on getting to know him better?
- Am I more concerned with how he is feeling about me rather than determining how I feel about him?

A fear of losing him has more to do with a low self-concept than a man's behavior. If a man is worthy of you and sees you as a potential mate, he will accept your standards.

Mistake #9: They Lack Confidence in Themselves and in Their Decision

When your self-esteem is low, you may not feel worthy of being abstinent until love grows. You may think that all you have to offer is sex. You don't feel worthy of love, so you do everything in your power to sabotage the relationship. You don't realize that you do have a lot to offer and that you do deserve the highest form of love there is. You may lack confidence in your decision to abstain and put love before sex if you:

- Continually change your mind about being abstinent.
- Are easily talked into sex.
- Are not clear about your reasons for abstaining and you don't express them with conviction.
- Don't feel comfortable being honest about your values.

As you grow as a woman, and you become very clear as to why you want to abstain, your confidence grows. Remember: you are absolutely justified in wanting to protect your mind, body, and soul from the damaging effects of having sex too soon. You deserve more than what a strictly physical relationship has to offer. You are worthy of true love that lasts forever.

Ask Yourself These Questions:

- Do I honestly believe that I have a right to say no to sex no matter how long I have been in the relationship?
- Am I comfortable with losing a man who won't accept my standards?
- Do I feel good about my desire to wait until I am committed, engaged, or married (choose one)?
- Do I feel comfortable expressing my sexual values to the men I date?

Mistake #10: They Deceive Themselves Into Thinking That They Have More of a Relationship Than They Really Do

Some women mistakenly believe that the relationship has more going for it than it really does. Men, whether conscious of it or not, sometimes do or say things that give the impression they are more into the woman than they are, or are interested in something more serious than they really are at that point. For example, he might say on the first few dates, "Wow—I've never met anyone quite like you." Or, "I haven't had this much fun with a woman in a long time." And then Poof! Her clothes are off and it's on! Then, when his feelings aren't sustained and he loses interest, she's devastated and confused. She reflects on all the things he said and did that gave her the impression it was a lock, and she can't believe it was all smoke and mirrors (he may have felt that way in the moment or he may have just been giving her a line—who knows). These women refuse to see the signs along the way, and they fall for a few lines that didn't mean all that much. Actions speak louder than words, and time is your best friend. Over time you will see the real him and, without sex in the way to cloud your feelings, you will observe how he treats you and others and you will see how both of your feelings truly develop.

You want to be in a relationship and feel close to someone. But sometimes you hear what you want to hear and see what you want to see. Then you are heartbroken when a year later he says, "I never actually *said* I loved you! I said I wanted to get married, but I never said *we* would get married!"

Brenda, 31, fell hard for Blake, 33 immediately:

Love Before Sex

"I wanted to get married so badly that I didn't see him for who he was. I was so taken by him, all I wanted to do was marry him. We had sex within a few weeks. I have never been promiscuous, but Blake said all the right things. When I met him, he was charming. He was everything I ever wanted. I lost my mind and my emotions. It is as though I got drunk on his words, his touch, his energy. He told me he wanted to take care of me. He asked all the right questions, the kinds of questions that get you excited about the possibility of a future together, like, "Where do you want to live? How many children do you want? What kind of house do you want?" These questions gave me the impression that he wanted these things with me, and they made me feel more comfortable about having sex with him. But after a couple of months, I found out he did not want those things with me, and he said he didn't feel like he misled me at all!"

Ask Yourself These Questions:

- Does he call me and ask me out regularly?
- Does he verbalize and express his love?
- Has he made it clear that I am the woman he wants—not just sexually but in every way?
- Is he consistent in his behavior towards me?
- What does my intuition tell me about his true feelings for me?

Whatever your circumstances, just becoming aware of your patterns can help you change the way you relate to men. You will begin to realize that you can create the relationship you want and that you don't have to be a victim of circumstance.

Chapter 15
Being a Great Lover for Life

There is no better sex than the sex you have with someone who loves you so much they want to spend the rest of their life with you. When you put *love before sex* you get the best of both worlds. You get a meaningful experience that *enhances* the relationship, not destroys it. Sex brings you closer together and deepens the level of intimacy you already share. It's the icing on the cake. Hope, 39, described it perfectly, "When my fiancé and I make love, it's so different from my past relationships. Mike looks into my eyes and I can see that he loves me by the way he looks at me, and his touch is so tender and loving. That doesn't mean we don't get passionate and even a little wild sometimes—but there's an *emotional* connection that had always been missing before."

Sex with love is different because your partner truly cares about you on a deeper level—therefore you feel safer, freer, more secure. You know that he has your best interests at heart and that he loves all of you, not just your body or what you can offer in the heat of the moment. You know that he will be there tomorrow and every day after that. You know that sex will only enhance the feelings and relationship you already have—it won't be the main event.

Love makes the experience richer and more satisfying. This doesn't mean that sex can't be raw, raunchy, racy, intense, and so on. You're free to do whatever turns you both on and it may not always be about candlelight and soft kisses. But the love that is present adds a new dimension that makes the whole experience better, especially afterwards, when you hold each other and you know you have the love of your life holding you and telling you how much he loves and adores you. It is my hope that you experience this type of love (and sex!) and that you never have to settle for anything less.

Tools for Love

You now have the tools you need to build lasting love. It all starts with you and the kind of woman you are. Be the kind of woman you want to be. Be a modern woman who knows who she is and what she wants, and who won't compromise her most precious values along the way. You now understand men and how the dating process works, and you can now approach your life with confidence. You should be very proud of yourself! You searched for wisdom and you took full responsibility for yourself and your life. You no longer have to settle for the weeds, or get bogged down with dead-end, dysfunctional relationships with men who are beneath you or who are just not right for you. Those days are over! It may not be easy to find the right person to share your life with, but once you apply the principles in this book, you will attract more men than ever, and you will be well-equipped to build a beautiful, lasting relationship that will bring you much joy and fulfillment.

Delaying Sexual Gratification

Delaying sexual gratification is not easy, for sure. But hopefully, as a result of reading this book, you have found a new inner confidence and strength that will give you the power to overcome the physical desire to give in to sex too soon, and that you will follow the guidelines in this book to the best of your ability. Read and re-read the book until it becomes a part of you, and then vow to yourself that you will wait until you have established love and commitment with the man of your choice (or engagement or marriage). Be selective and don't ever settle. Now that you know what you're doing you never have to settle! You can have the pick of the men out there because you have knowledge that gives you power.

Be a Great Lover

Once you do become sexual with someone, make up for lost time! Strive to be a great lover by having an open, positive attitude. Be flexible and willing to try new things. Do your best to please your partner, and he'll try to please you. But don't ever do anything you don't feel comfortable doing. It's always okay to say no. If you experienced sexual trauma as a child or young woman, work through these experiences with a therapist and do everything you can to become free of the emotional and psychological burdens they create. There is no reason why you can't overcome these past situations and be a healthy woman with a healthy sex life, free of traumatic triggers that hold you back. It's up to you to take control of your emotional and psychological development and to overcome these things. Don't let them control your life and prevent you from enjoying life to the fullest.

Your New Journey

I hope you have found this book to be enlightening and inspirational. I hope that you are able to take the concepts and apply them wholeheartedly in your own life. If you have a pattern of getting involved with Mr. Wrong, and are sick of the serial monogamy game, I hope that you feel a renewed sense of excitement about breaking that pattern so that you can finally create true love in your life. Whatever your circumstances, I hope you'll apply the principles and create the life you've always wanted. This journey requires a lot of courage and self-discipline. But mostly you have to want to be loved and cherished more than anything. Your desire for a beautiful relationship with a good man will be the driving force and it will guide your choices. Be patient and hang in there... it will all come together in time.

Please write to me and tell me your success stories. I am excited about your journey ahead and would love to share in your experiences. I wish you all the love and happiness in the world.

About the Author

Laurie Gelfand, Ph.D. (aka "Dr. G.") is a life/relationship coach with a Ph.D. in clinical psychology. She holds popular seminars and workshops on topics related to relationships and personal growth.

She has appeared on dozens of national TV and radio shows, including Montel, CNN, The O'Reilly Factor, USA Live, and Good Day New York. Dr. G. has published two books. Her first book, *If It's Love You Want, Why Settle for Just Sex* (Prima, 1996), was published in several languages under her maiden name, Laurie Langford. Her second book is *The Big Talk: Talking to Your Child About Sex and Dating* (Wiley & Sons, 1998).

Dr. G. is happily married to her husband Michael, and they reside in both Rancho Santa Fe, CA. and Los Angeles, CA. with their 3 dogs: Maggie, Charlie, and Lenny.

Laurie Gelfand, Ph.D.
P.O. Box 9262
Rancho Santa Fe, CA 92067
(858) 756-0640
talktodrg@gmail.com
www.lovebeforesex.com

Love Before Sex

You might also be interested in purchasing the companion journal and/or workbook, which can be purchased from the website. They are designed to go hand-in-hand with the book, offering you exercises and insights that will aid you in your journey to building true love.

Made in the USA
San Bernardino, CA
21 April 2014